Discovery
CHANNEL
PRO CYCLING TEAM

TEACH YOUR KID
TO RIDE A BIKE

MARK RIEDY

For complete team coverage and cycling news on the Discovery Channel® Pro Cycling Team,
visit http://team.discovery.com and http://thepaceline.com.

Notice

This book is intended as a reference volume only, not as a medical manual. The information given here is designed to help you make informed decisions about your health. It is not intended as a substitute for any treatment that may have been prescribed by your doctor. If you suspect that you have a medical problem, we urge you to seek competent medical help.

Mention of specific companies, organizations, or authorities in this book does not imply endorsement by the publisher, nor does mention of specific companies, organizations, or authorities imply that they endorse this book.

Internet addresses and telephone numbers given in this book were accurate at the time it went to press.

Rodale books may be purchased for business or promotional use or for special sales. For information, please write to: Special Markets Department, Rodale Inc., 733 Third Avenue, New York, NY 10017

Printed in the United States of America
Rodale Inc. makes every effort to use acid-free ∞, recycled paper ♲.

Cover and interior photography credits are on page 148.

Cover design by Joanna Williams
Interior design by Gavin Robinson

Library of Congress Cataloging-in-Publication Data

Riedy, Mark.
  Discovery Channel pro cycling team teach your kid to ride a bike / by Mark Riedy.
       p.   cm.
  Includes index.
  ISBN-13 978-1-59486-398-1   paperback
  ISBN-10 1-59486-398-9   paperback
  1. Cycling for children.   2. Cycling—Safety measures.   I. Title.
GV1057.2.R54 2006
796.6083—dc22   2006011212

Distributed to the book trade by Holtzbrinck Publishers

2   4   6   8   10   9   7   5   3   1   paperback

RODALE
LIVE YOUR WHOLE LIFE™

We inspire and enable people to improve their lives and the world around them
For more of our products visit **rodalestore.com** or call 800-848-4735

CONTENTS

FOREWORD

By Chris Carmichael

There are some childhood photos every parent takes, including the one with the beaming smile from behind the handlebars of a child's first bicycle. Your parents have one of you, and you're going to take one of your child, too. Learning to ride a bicycle is a rite of passage, and for many children it's one of the first skills they will consciously remember learning.

There's no feeling quite like the first moment you realize you're riding a bicycle all by yourself—that Mom or Dad just let go and you're on your own, really doing it. My son, Connor, is 4 years old, and he loves to ride his bike. I'll never forget the moment he realized he was balanced on top of two wheels; I was running alongside but he was on his own, and he looked up at me with a look of amazement and bewilderment. I could almost see the gears turning in his little head: *If Dad is running alongside, then who's holding on to the seat?* That's when his eyes sprung wide open. He had done it! After a week of falling over in the grass, he was up and going. Of course, he hadn't mastered turning or stopping yet, so he tipped over a few moments later, but within another 30 minutes he was cruising around the grassy field like a champion.

A bicycle can change a child's life. It provides a means to expand horizons and explore the world, or at least the neighborhood. It's also a fun way to establish healthy habits that can carry all the way through adulthood. Your children may never have any interest in cycling as an organized sport, and that's okay, but getting them out of the house and onto a bike can help them become better athletes in whatever sport they choose. Riding a bike as a child helps to develop *proprioception,* or balance and body awareness, as well as reflexes and coordination, all of which play crucial roles in sports such as baseball, football, hockey, basketball, and tennis.

A bicycle can also provide a strong lesson in responsibility. When I was young, my father showed me how to clean my bike and told me how important it was to care for things that were mine. That bike was really the first thing I associated as *being* mine, and it meant everything to me. I cleaned it, made sure it was put away, and tinkered with the chain and pedals and fenders. As I later learned as a bike racer and preached as a coach, a clean bike is a fast bike, and attention to detail means you're always prepared.

Perhaps most of all, a bicycle gives a child independence and freedom. I realize that the world may not be as safe as it was when I used to spend all day wandering through neighborhoods by myself as a kid, but riding a bicycle to and from school, or down to the library or to a friend's house, is an experience of traveling alone, even if it's only for a short distance. At the appropriate age, a little bit of control over getting from here to there can have a big impact on a child's self-confidence and independence.

But when you boil it all down to its essence, learning to ride a bicycle is about fun. It's about the wind in your face and the warm sun on your back, and the freedom to go wherever your legs can carry you. And, of course, it's also about that photo.

Chris Carmichael and his family hit the trail as a group.

ACKNOWLEDGMENTS

The first time I took my 2-year-old daughter Rio out for a ride around the neighborhood, I belted her into a little seat perched atop the handlebars of a hybrid bike. When I asked her if she was ready to go home, she screamed, "No," with equal parts joy and mischief. "I want to go!" Although I've ridden hundreds of thousands of miles with fun and fascinating people in some of the most beautiful places on earth, that was surely the best moment I've ever had on two wheels. Rio's continual laughter and energy have made my life better than I could've ever imagined.

Neither Rio nor this book nor my life as it is today would be possible with out the love and support of my wife, Rachel. She keeps my head on straight and inspires me to do great things.

Thanks also to my mother, Ruth Robenalt, who spent countless hours and thousands of dollars taking me to cycling events, paying for my equipment, and coaching me through rough patches. Thanks Mom.

While he probably didn't pull in enough to cover the cost of a spare inner tube on this project, Jeremy Katz proved to be more than just my agent; he was and is a continual source of guidance.

At Rodale, Heidi Rodale, Marilyn Hauptly, and Emily Williams were patient, incredibly easy to work with, and pushed me to do great work.

Outside my immediate family, Brian Fiske and Christine Vardaros played a dramatic role in helping with the nuts and bolts of assembling this book. Thanks for the hard work, guys.

PJ Rabice of CSE proved to be a crucial link between the Discovery Channel Pro Cycling Team and the effort to write this book. Thanks also to the entire staff at the Discovery Channel and the Discovery Channel Pro Cycling Team for their efforts.

Others that helped either with information, insight, or support include Steve Madden and the entire team at *Bicycling* magazine,

Chris Carmichael of Carmichael Training Systems, Dean Golich and Jim Rutberg of Carmichael Training Systems, Mike Sinyard, Sean Sullivan, and the rest of the people at Specialized Bicycle Components in Morgan Hill, California.

On a personal level, Ben Capron; Dr. Allen Roland; Liz, John, Ben, and Juiliana Cleaveland; Dan Koeppel; Matt Phillips; Mike Cushionbury; Bill Strickland; Loren Mooney; Michael Frank; Tim Parr; Mike Geraci; Chris Denny; Ben Hewitt; Todd Toth; Kevin Franks; and Jim Startt proved to be a constant source of support, encouragement, and laughter.

Finally, this book would never have gotten out the door without a steady stream of Taylor Maid Farms Red Rooster's French Roast.

PART I

· ·

SAFETY

Riding Is and Should Always Be Fun

· ·

"I ended up racing my bike for a living, making a career out of it," says the Discovery Channel Pro Cycling Team's George Hincapie, the only racer to ride beside Lance Armstrong in each of his seven Tour de France victories. "But what got me hooked on riding was that it was fun and adventure that I've only ever found on a bike."

You probably remember the exhilaration and freedom of hopping on a two-wheeler and speeding off down the block as one of the most powerful and enduring memories of your childhood. Yet, without proper guidance and a working understanding of the bicycle and the correct way to operate it, your child's experience on two wheels could end in frustration and, possibly, injury. To ensure that your young riders have a safe and fun introduction to the bicycle, be sure to spend some time instructing them on the basics of bicycle mechanics, skills, and the rules and regulations of the road before turning them loose with their bikes.

These key strategies will make your experience safer and more rewarding:

- Get heavily involved with the purchase of the bike—make sure your young one is getting a bike that fits and that is designed for the type of riding she is most likely to do.

- Ensure that she also has the correct equipment, such as a helmet, shoes, shorts, and gloves.

- Spend time talking with her about the bike's components and how they function.

- Give her a full briefing on the rules and laws of the road.

WHEN SHOULD A CHILD LEARN TO RIDE A BIKE?

Like most things in life, there's no perfect age for a child to learn how to ride. Head to the park on a sunny Sunday and you'll see children as young as 3 or 4 years old sprinting away from their parents on 10- or 12-inch-wheeled bikes. Because all children—all people for that matter—mature at different rates, it's best to not focus on your child's age when considering whether he's ready to ride or not. Instead, keep the following list of crucial indicators in mind.

SIZE *Most kids have an inseam of at least 17 inches when they begin the process of learning to ride. That height ensures that they can easily straddle a 12-inch-wheeled bike. Of course, if your child is ready to ride before he is tall enough to ride a 12-inch-wheeled bike, there are any number of bikes built for smaller children. Beware of the smaller, less expensive bikes, though, as they often use fixed gears (because the rear cog has no freewheel, there's no possibility of coasting) and lower-quality components. Most often, it's better just to wait until your child is a little taller and can ride a higher-quality bike.*
COORDINATION *When children try to learn how to ride before they're physically ready, it's likely to be more frustrating than*

KEEP IT FUN

What is cycling if not fun? The reason you're probably interested in teaching your kids or other young ones how to ride is that you've found cycling to be fun. Sure, it's a healthy and, in some cases, life-changing experience, but above all, riding is fun. Everything you do with your child on a bike should have the ultimate goal of having a blast.

Here are some pointers that will help ensure a fun ride.

Lead by Example If you're having fun, it's easy for your kids to follow in your footsteps, but if you're stressed out, not paying attention to their needs, or acting somewhat less than excited about the outing, it'll be impossible for your kids or anyone else to enjoy themselves around you.

. . . .

fun. If you're having trouble deciding whether your young one is ready to learn to ride or not, there are some easy tests you can have him do to check his physical maturity. Have your child hop on one leg, walk while balancing on a parking curb, or squat down to the floor while standing on one foot with the other foot outstretched. If he can do any of these things with relative confidence, he's more than likely ready to ride; if not, it is probably best to wait a little longer.

DESIRE *It seems pretty obvious, but if your child doesn't really want to learn how to ride, he's not likely to. If he's continually bugging you to buy him a bike, trying to straddle an older sibling's bike, or even hopping on neighborhood friends' bikes and trying to ride on his own, it's time to get him rolling. But if your kids are more interested in reading books, kicking a soccer ball, or playing with dolls, wait until they show some level of interest.*

AWARENESS *Even if he's only starting out by riding down the driveway, it's essential that your child have some under-standing that riding too fast, riding dangerously, or not paying attention to people, other bikes, or vehicles that may be in the way could result in serious injury.*

. . . .

Communicate, Communicate, Communicate Providing details on every aspect of the ride—from distance to the time it will take and the sites you can expect to see—will help remove many of the uncertainties of riding. That will allow your kids to be more relaxed and happy. One great way to do this is to hand out a map with ride directions for every ride. This way, even if young ones become lost, they have a way to ask others for directions home or back to the start of the ride. (Be sure they understand that reading and riding are two things best done separately.)

Give Them the Support System They Need to Enjoy Riding Whether it's making sure they have the right gear, pumping up their tires, giving them an understanding of the rules of the road, or outfitting them with the right skills, the better you prepare your kids, the more fun they'll have while cycling.

Be Ready for Unexpected Events When does anything in life ever go according to plan? Rarely. So, have a loose plan, one that can accommodate last-minute changes or disruptions. Oftentimes, a simple mechanical problem can ruin an otherwise perfect ride; but with a flexible plan in place, it's more likely that at least some riders can have some fun on the outing.

Keep It Realistic Make sure that the rides that you plan are realistic for the age, fitness, and skill set of everyone involved. Nothing can sour a child on riding faster than a ride that she's not mentally and physically equipped to handle. If there is a big disparity in age, fitness, or skills of the riders in a given group, consider splitting the group into more equal halves.

Check In Once you are out on the road or trail, be sure to check in at consistent intervals, and have a "sweeper" at the back of every ride to be sure that nobody is lost or left behind. Monitoring the condition of your young riders will make it easier for you to encourage those who need it and, if necessary, to alter the ride itinerary.

RULES OF THE ROAD

Cyclists face the same dangers as other drivers. They share space with moving cars, motorcycles, and pedestrians, and they may encounter

Whether riding on or off-road, your young ones should have complete knowledge of all safety rules.

any number of other hazards. But cycling requires an entirely different set of skills than driving a car. The following seven traffic management strategies are essential for young cyclists who may have not developed the necessary skills, confidence, or intuition to handle themselves safely in traffic.

ASSUME YOU'RE INVISIBLE

Being the smallest, quietest, lightest vehicle on the road means that you have to assume that you're completely invisible to all other traffic. That means assuming that a car will turn in front of you or that a pedestrian will suddenly dart into your path. Watch a vehicle's front wheels: They telegraph a turn even when the motorist forgets to use a signal.

MAKE YOURSELF VISIBLE

As a cyclist, assuming you're invisible is half the battle. The other half is doing everything you can to be seen. This includes wearing yellow, red, or other brightly colored clothing. Consider using a small, flashing light even during daylight hours; today's ultra-bright and amazingly lightweight LED lights are one of the most amazing safety advances of the past 20 years. When riding in low light or darkness, front and rear lights are mandatory. Good lights have longer burn times and are less expensive than ever, so there's no reason not to have them.

GO WITH THE FLOW

Regardless of what you may have been told, the correct way to ride is *with* the flow of traffic. The vehicle code in all 50 states recognizes a bicycle as a motor vehicle, meaning that you are legally bound to ride just as if you were a car, truck, or motorcycle. Go with the flow of traffic in all places and at all times.

KEEP RIGHT

In nearly all situations, there is no reason to ride on the left side of the white line that divides the edge of the roadway from the shoulder. Road hazards such as gravel, glass, potholes, metal grates, or other debris could prevent you from riding to the right of the white line. In that case, it may be necessary to move to the left of the white line, but time spent in the active traffic lane should be minimized at all costs.

AVOID HEAVILY TRAFFICKED ROADS

For a cyclist, the road less traveled is the road best traveled. Staying away from main roads makes riding safer for you and less frustrating for motorists.

THE GOLDEN RULE

When riding in traffic, do unto others as you would have them do unto you. That means *not* weaving in and out of traffic, splitting lanes, running stop signs, sprinting through yellow lights, hopping curbs, or turning without a signal. Remember: You point directly with your left arm for a left turn and with your right for a right turn. Hold your left arm down with palm facing rearward to indicate a stop. Motorists will feel more comfortable around and respectful of cyclists who communicate their intentions.

BE COURTEOUS

Finally and above all else, be courteous to all other motorists and pedestrians. Provoking a motorist, even when he is clearly at fault, will often cause a situation to escalate far beyond what is reasonable given the circumstances. It's also a disservice to fellow cyclists to be seen as a menace; your actions will reflect badly on all cyclists. So, be polite, even when you've clearly been the victim of poor driving. If a situation mandates it, contact the police and report the offending motorist's license plate number.

RULES OF THE TRAIL

It may be tough to remember when zinging down a choice chunk of singletrack, but the hard fact is that one wrong move on even the most mundane trail can put you or another rider in danger. Add to that the fact that very few trails are built in close proximity to a hospital and the gravity of the situation only increases. "My wife, who is a professional mountain biker, and I spend a lot of time in the winter out on the trails around our home in Durango," says Discovery Channel Team rider Tom Danielson. "Yet we're always aware of the dangers and we have a plan in the event that one of us gets hurt."

CRASHING: NOT IF . . . WHEN

Even the absolute best riders in the world crash, so there's no question that one of your young ones will crash someday too. So be sure that they are always mentally prepared to fall. When you *expect* to crash, you're ready to crash, and when you're *ready* to crash, you stand a much better chance of rolling out of your fall unscathed.

DON'T RUN OUT OF TALENT

Know how far your skills, your equipment, and the conditions will take you, and don't exceed that limit. If you and your young riders stay within the limits of talent, conditions, and equipment, the result will be fewer falls, even in the most challenging terrain.

STOP WHEN SCARED

Any rider should stop to assess any terrain that looks close to the limit of their skills and equipment. This will minimize falls and encourage a rider to test his limits in the safest way possible.

....
IMBA'S RULES OF THE TRAIL
....

Founded in 1988, the International Mountain Biking Association (IMBA) created the Rules of the Trail as one of their first actions. In the intervening 15-plus years, these rules have been adopted by land managers throughout the United States. Follow them, and you're almost sure to have a fun, safe ride that doesn't damage the trail.

Ride on Open Trails Only

Respect trail and road closures (ask if uncertain); avoid trespassing on private land; obtain permits or other authorization as may be required. Federal and state wilderness areas are closed to cycling. The way you ride will influence trail management decisions and policies.

Leave No Trace

Be sensitive to the dirt beneath you. Recognize different types of soils and trail construction; practice low-impact cycling. Wet and muddy trails are more vulnerable to damage. When the trail is soft, consider other riding options. This also means staying on existing trails and not creating new ones. Don't cut switchbacks. Be sure to pack out at least as much as you pack in.

Control Your Bicycle

Inattention for even a second can cause problems. Obey all bicycle speed regulations and recommendations.

....

GO SLOWER ON UNKNOWN TRAILS

The second time any rider covers a given trail, she will ride it much faster because she will have taken note of any harsh drop, unexpected corner, or other extreme hazard. The first time on any trail or terrain should be taken at no more than half the speed a rider feels that she could take it at her limit.

Always Yield the Trail

Let your fellow trail users know you're coming. A friendly greeting or bell is considerate and works well; don't startle others. Show your respect when passing by slowing to a walking pace or even stopping. Anticipate other trail users around corners or in blind spots. Yielding means slow down, establish communication, be prepared to stop if necessary, and pass safely.

Never Scare Animals

All animals are startled by an unannounced approach, a sudden movement, or a loud noise. This can be dangerous for you, others, and the animals. Give animals extra room and time to adjust to you. When passing horses, use special care and follow directions from the horseback riders (ask if uncertain). Running cattle and disturbing wildlife is a serious offense. Leave gates as you found them, or as marked.

Plan Ahead

Know your equipment, your ability, and the area in which you are riding—and prepare accordingly. Be self-sufficient at all times, keep your equipment in good repair, and carry necessary supplies for changes in weather or other conditions. A well-executed trip is a satisfaction to you and not a burden to others. Always wear a helmet and appropriate safety gear.

See www.IMBA.com for more information.

DON'T RIDE BLIND

Regardless of how many times you or one of your young riders has covered a trail, it's dangerous and disrespectful to others to take a blind corner at full speed. Short of having ESP, there's simply no way to know whether there's another rider or a natural hazard waiting around the corner.

RIDE THE RIGHT RIDE

While you can't have a different bike for every trail condition, it's important that you ride a bike that is designed and configured optimally for the conditions. For rough, rugged, or extreme conditions, full suspension and wider tires are appropriate. For mellow fire roads, a hardtail with less aggressive tires might be all that's necessary.

FOLLOW THE LEADER

On any group ride, make sure the faster riders are at the front of the group and the slower, less skilled riders are at the back. This will help to keep anyone from feeling pushed to ride beyond his skill level.

KNOW THE BIKE

As with a car or motorcycle, a general working knowledge of the bicycle makes hitting the road or trail much safer; any rider who knows how to spot a worn or defective part is much more likely to avoid a midride breakdown or catastrophic accident. Every young rider should be able to perform the following preride safety check on her bike.

Frame and Fork Thanks to digital design, modeling, testing, and vastly improved materials, today's frames are stronger and more durable than ever. Yet, every frame and fork can fail due to fatigue or a crash. Between rides, wipe down the bike's frame and fork, checking carefully for any cracks or inconsistencies in tube shape. With carbon fiber frames, a soft spot indicates that the tube has been compromised and is no longer safe. Barring an accident or a hard fall, the frame and fork should last for years and years of riding.

Brakes A bike will have one of three types of brakes: caliper, cantilever, or disc. Most road bikes have caliper or cantilever brakes, and the most likely problem is pad wear. Check the brake pads frequently to ensure that there is enough rubber remaining to stop the bike safely. If the pads appear to be heavily worn or damaged, replace them immediately. The proliferation of mountain bikes in the past decade has meant that disc brakes are now found on many mountain, touring, and cyclocross bikes. If the bike has disc brakes, check the disc and frame or fork-mounted calipers occasionally to ensure that the mounting bolts are snug. Roughly every 100 hours of use, have a trained mechanic check the disc pads and the general functionality of the system.

Chain, Derailleurs, and Shifters As the bicycle's transmission, the chain, derailleurs, and shifters will need more attention than the bicycle's other components. Between rides, wipe the chain with a rag, apply a light, bicycle-specific lubricant, and carefully check for wear. Even in clean and dry conditions, the chain will need to be replaced after 100 hours of use on a road bike and after 50 hours of use on a mountain bike. As with the chain, the front and rear derailleurs should be wiped between rides and examined for damage or excessive wear.

Crank The crank is often a point of failure because it's the component that transfers the input from the rider's legs to the bicycle. As with the windshield of a car, even the smallest crack in a crank arm will eventually spell failure for the component. Should you spot any damage to the crank or associated components, take it to a trained mechanic for further examination. Barring a major accident or impact, a well-designed crank should last for the lifetime of the bike.

Pedals These components suffer endless abuse and need careful inspection and maintenance. Clean and lube the pedals on a regular basis, checking for loose bearings and cracks or, if the bike has clipless pedals, a faulty retention mechanism. Similarly, keep the pedal's cleats (which are bolted to the bottom of cycling-specific shoes) snug and clean.

Handlebar and Stem With just a few moving parts, the most likely safety-related issue with a stem and handlebar is failure due to fatigue.

(continued on page 14)

ANATOMY OF A BICYCLE

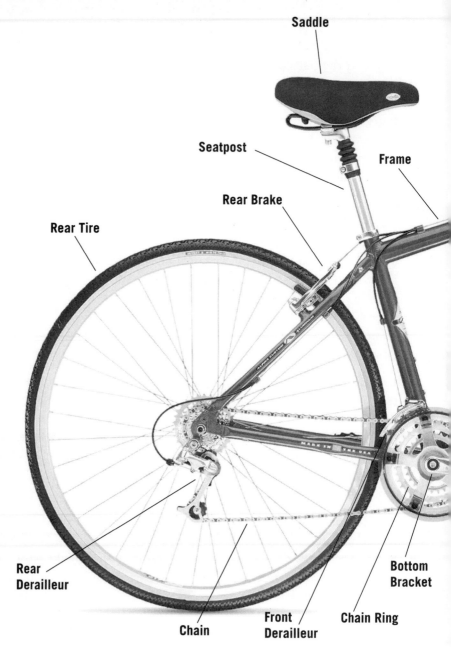

Saddle

Seatpost

Frame

Rear Brake

Rear Tire

Rear
Derailleur

Chain

Front
Derailleur

Chain Ring

Bottom
Bracket

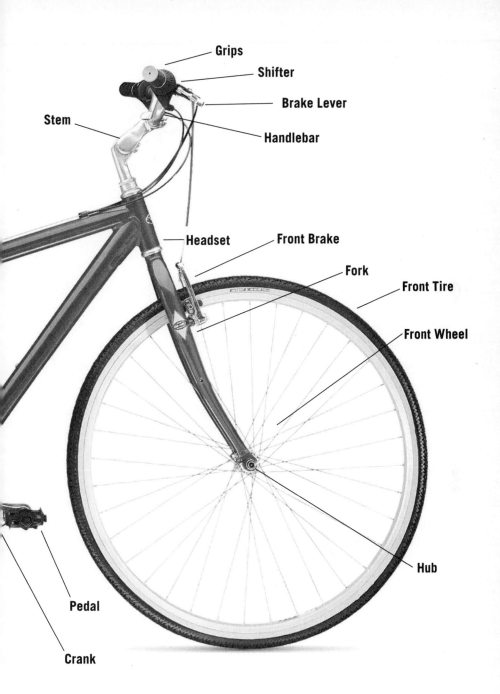

Grips

Shifter

Brake Lever

Stem

Handlebar

Headset

Front Brake

Fork

Front Tire

Front Wheel

Hub

Pedal

Crank

When washing the bike or taping the handlebars, check for straightness and for small cracks or other damage. While a good handlebar and stem should last the lifetime of a bike, a crash or even an accidental drop can damage either component to the point of replacement.

Saddle and Post A quality seatpost is likely never to wear out, but even the best saddles need frequent examination for damage or rider-induced wear. Check the saddle rails for straightness (they can be damaged even by a bike simply falling over) and the saddle cover for rips or tears. Also, notice whether the saddle's foam or gel padding is retaining its original spring and shape. A saddle with compromised or inadequate padding needs to be replaced immediately to avoid discomfort or saddle sores.

Tires and Tubes Flat tires have been the cause of more ruined rides than perhaps any other culprit. To avoid punctures out on the road or trail, inspect the tires frequently, looking for cuts in the tread or sidewall. While small cuts won't likely result in a flat, tires without wear are always safer and less likely to "flat" than those with wear. Replace the tires early and often to avoid a flat or worse.

Wheels The rolling bedrock of any bike, wheels need frequent care and attention. Wipe down the wheels between rides with a dry cloth, checking the rims for straightness and roundness (a wheel that's out of round is actually worse than one that's not straight). Check the spokes for gouges or wear. Grip the rim in your hand and move it from side to side, checking the bearings for play. Spin the rear wheel and listen to the freehub for a dry or grinding noise. At minimum, have the wheels trued by a professional mechanic after every 100 hours of use for a road bike and 50 hours of use for a mountain bike.

HELMET FIT

According to the Bicycle Helmet Safety Institute, careful, experienced cyclists average one crash every 4,500 miles. Though your child may be careful, he is far from experienced—so he's going to crash a lot more often. A proper-fitting, Consumer Product Safety Commission (CPSC)–certified helmet could prevent 85 percent of cyclists' head injuries. And there's good news: You don't need to buy the most expensive helmet to protect your child's noggin—CPSC–certified helmets cost as little as $20. To ensure that a helmet is certified always check its liner for a sticker that indicates CPSC compliance. Regardless of price, the CPSC certification ensures that the helmet you strap on to your young rider is designed for maximum safety and protection. How do helmets help? Most bike helmets are made of expanded polystyrene foam (the same foam found in picnic coolers) connected to a tough, hard plastic shell. In a fall, the foam crushes to absorb the impact and protect your skull.

Obviously, the materials used to make a helmet are important, but even more crucial is the way the helmet fits—as well as how it's held on your head. After all, if the helmet doesn't stay in place during a fall, it will offer little or no protection.

QUICK-AND-EASY HELMET FIT TEST

1. With the helmet in place and the strap snug, but not tight against your child's chin, push up and back on the front of the helmet. If it moves back far enough to show your child's forehead, try:

>   Finding a smaller size helmet

>   Snugging up the chin strap

>   Swapping interior pads to a thicker set (multiple thicknesses of pads are usually included with any helmet).

2. Next, give the back of the helmet a slight lift. If it rotates down and forward to cover your child's eyes, try:

>   Finding a smaller size helmet

>   Snugging the rear strap and/or retention device

>   Swapping interior pads for a thicker set.

3. Place your hands on each side of the middle of the helmet and gently shake it from side to side. If it slips or slides excessively, try:

>   Finding a smaller size helmet

>   Swapping the pads in the center of the helmet for a thicker set

>   Adjusting the rear retention device

>   Snugging the straps.

4. After tweaking the helmet as described in steps 1 through 3, your child's helmet should sit snugly on her head when she opens her mouth as wide as possible. If this causes her pain or stretches the helmet straps, try:

Lengthening the chin strap slightly

Loosening the rear retention device slightly.

Be sure that your child's helmet fits properly and be sure she wears it when she rides—in most places it's the law.

A FEW MORE HELMET FACTS

Never, ever buy a used helmet. There's just no way to know how old it is, who used it, how much it was used, or whether it's been worn in an accident.

Similarly, replace any helmet that has been worn during a crash. The downside to today's amazingly lightweight and well-ventilated helmets is that they are designed to withstand a single fall. In protecting the skull, the foam is often compressed to the point that it can no longer absorb any force.

Replace the helmet every 2 or 3 years at least. The expanded polystyrene foam from which most helmets are constructed degrades over time and slowly loses its protective ability.

While less expensive bicycle helmets must pass the same CPSC standards as professional quality helmets, the less expensive helmets often do not offer the same level of cooling. As a rule, the more vents a helmet has, the cooler the wearer's head will be and the more expensive the helmet will be.

ROAD BIKE FIT

FRAME

In the past decade, the formula for calculating traditional road fit has gone out the window, thanks to an influx of new frame designs and technologies. Yet the old method of determining the correct length of the seat tube by measuring your inseam will give you a great baseline figure to use when shopping. Have your child stand with her bare feet 6 inches apart, and measure her inseam from crotch to floor. Multiply that number by 0.65 to find her traditional road frame size. For example, if your teenager has a 28-inch inseam, you would use a traditional 18-inch-tall frame as the baseline.

With knowledge of the correct traditional frame size in hand, head to as many bike shops as you possibly can. Due to the lack of standardization, you'll need to rely on the dealer's sales staff to point you in the right direction. Trust your and your child's own judgment, though—within reason, the best bike is ultimately the one that feels right for the rider.

SADDLE HEIGHT

Although finding the proper bike fit is truly a system, where every measurement and change to it affects every other measurement, the single most important dimension when fitting your bicycle is saddle height. There are a number of competing (and overly complex) formulas for computing the precise saddle height of a given rider on a particular bike, but it's very easy to get a near-perfect fit with this simple method, which has been used for decades:

1. With his feet bare, have your child sit on the saddle of the bike with his legs fully extended and not resting on the pedals.

2. Tweak the saddle's height until there is roughly 5 millimeters of clearance between his heel and the pedal at the bottom of the stroke. (If he has long feet in proportion to his height, you should set the saddle slightly higher than 5 millimeters.)

3. Once you have the height dialed, have him slip into his cycling shoes, hop on the bike, and pedal. The correct height is the one at which your child's knee is slightly bent at the very bottom of the pedal stroke. You'll know if you've set the saddle too high if you can see or feel his hips rocking from side to side.

4. Out on the road, you will likely need to make slight adjustments until the saddle height is perfect. Remember to make small changes, of no more than 2 millimeters at a time, in order to avoid injury.

SADDLE FORE/AFT AND TILT

The saddle's fore/aft position relative to the pedals determines both the reach to the handlebar and the relative mechanical advantage a rider has on the pedals. For example, a saddle that is moved farther back over the pedals allows a rider to produce more power, but it also increases the overall reach to the handlebars. The best position is one that balances reach and position over the bottom bracket to allow for the best blend of power, comfort, and control.

As for tilt, the best, most comfortable position is level to the ground.

Tilting the saddle slightly downward will cause you to put too much weight on the rider's arms, while even a slightly upward tilt will likely cause some discomfort where she sits.

REACH

The combined length of the bike frame's top tube and stem make up the total reach of the bike. Because an individual's reach is affected by his body type, flexibility, and desire for more or less comfort or performance, there is ultimately no single hard-and-fast formula for calculating precise reach. Still, you can find a good middle-of-the-road starting point with the following formula: The hub of the front wheel should be obscured by the handlebars and your child's elbows should be slightly bent if he is sitting comfortably in the saddle with his hands on the tops of the brake levers.

HANDLEBAR WIDTH AND HEIGHT

There used to be very few options as far as handlebar types and styles go, but thanks to the introduction of carbon fiber handlebars, which can be extensively molded and shaped, there is now a virtually limitless array of choices. The correct width for the handlebars is slightly wider than the rider's shoulders. Handlebar height is determined by the desire for comfort versus performance. The lower the handlebars, the more aerodynamic the rider will be—but he's also less likely to be comfortable. Experiment with various heights to find the best balance for your young rider's style of riding.

MOUNTAIN BIKE FIT

Because mountain bike frames are more compact than those used on the road, and thanks to the rough-and-tumble nature of off-road riding, proper fit is a bit easier to achieve and is less sensitive than with a road bike. Still, experimenting before you buy is absolutely essential.

FRAME

The single most important rule when sizing yourself or a young rider to a mountain bike is that you want the smallest frame possible that still provides enough saddle height, stem height, and top tube length.

A smaller frame is lighter and more rigid and provides a maximum amount of clearance for emergency maneuvers or dismounts.

SADDLE HEIGHT

The difference between good road and mountain saddle heights is that, thanks to the jostling from the trail and the body English necessary for good handling, a rider needs to have slightly less leg extension on a mountain bike.

1. With her feet bare, have your child sit on the saddle of the bike with her legs fully extended and not resting on the pedals.

2. Tweak the saddle's height until there is roughly 5 millimeters of clearance between her heel and the pedal at the bottom of the stroke. (If she has long feet in proportion to her height, you should set the saddle slightly higher than 5 millimeters.)

3. Once you have the height dialed, have her slip into her cycling shoes, hop on the bike, and pedal. The correct height is the one at which her knee is more than slightly bent at the bottom of the pedal stroke. You'll know that the saddle is set too high if she feels that she is "reaching" for the pedals at any point in the pedal stroke and if she feels that she's not able to transfer all her power to the pedals when riding on rough or bumpy terrain.

4. Out on the trail, you will often need to make adjustments to saddle height, so it's best to be sure that your bike has a quick-release seat collar that allows for speedy, tool-free adjustments. Rough or extremely steep trails often require a drop in saddle height of between 1 and 6 inches; smooth dirt or paved roads will allow you to raise the saddle slightly higher than normal for improved power transfer. More than with road saddle height, you'll need to experiment to find the best balance of power, comfort, and control for your child.

SADDLE FORE/AFT AND TILT

As with road bikes, a mountain bike saddle's fore/aft position relative to the pedals determines both the reach to the handlebar and the relative mechanical advantage that a rider has on the pedals. On a mountain bike, it's best to have the saddle a little farther forward than on a road bike, to allow a rider to distribute her weight more evenly across the bike and to pedal with a higher cadence.

Just as on a road bike, the best, most comfortable angle for the saddle is dead level to the ground. Tilting the saddle slightly down will force your child to put too much weight on her arms, causing fatigue and a loss of control, while even a slightly upward tilt will likely cause some discomfort and an uneven pedal stroke.

HANDLEBAR REACH AND HEIGHT

On a mountain bike, the rider's position is significantly more upright than on a typical road bike. This allows the rider to be positioned in the center of the bike for even weight distribution and maximum control. When fitting a rider on a mountain bike, try to experiment with the height of the handlebars by swapping headset spacers and trying stems with varying amounts of rise and reach. The best position is one where the rider feels completely comfortable and in control, yet has enough of a bend in her lower back to ensure efficient transfer of power.

HANDLEBAR WIDTH

There is a wide range of handlebar widths for mountain biking and no definitive formula for calculating the proper size for a given rider. Generally speaking, more aggressive off-road riding, such as freeride and downhill, calls for wider bars, the widest of which are 28 inches from end to end. The quick turns and narrow trails used for general trail riding and cross-country racing favor narrower bars, usually in the 22- to 23-inch range. If you have no idea what's best for you, the best place to begin is with a 25-inch-wide bar that features a slight rise. Note that these dimensions are typical for adult mountain bikes; your local bike shop can help you find the size that's right for a younger rider.

PROPER ATTIRE

For many parents, agreeing on an outfit and getting a young one out the door and off to school is a daily challenge, so convincing him to suit up in performance-oriented cycling gear is probably not going to happen. Pick your battles with the essential items and give way where safety is not an issue.

Helmet No negotiating here. In most states it's simply a law that anyone under 18 years of age has to wear a helmet at all times while riding a bicycle. Don't feel that you have to spend a million dollars to get a lid that protects; any helmet sold in any shop in America is tested to the same CPSC standard. More expensive helmets will be lighter and better ventilated, but any CPSC–approved helmet will protect your child in a fall.

Shorts/Padded Liner Even if your young rider is dead set against wearing Lycra shorts, he can slip on a snug-fitting, padded liner and wear his jeans over top of it. He'll still benefit from the best features of cycling-specific shorts—namely, padding and moisture wicking—without looking "like a dork."

Jersey In temperate weather, little more than a T-shirt is actually necessary. If conditions are cool or breezy, a moisture-wicking fabric such as Nike Dri-FIT or Patagonia Capilene will help keep your young rider from catching a cold. For mountain biking, there are any number of loose-fitting, motocross-inspired jerseys that most young boys will be stoked to have.

Gloves With the wide range of gloves on the market—long-finger, short-finger, even carbon fiber–encrusted downhill mitts—you should have no trouble getting your young rider to slip on a pair of protective, sweat-absorbing gloves. Key features to look for include kid-friendly sizing, a protective but not bulky palm, a breathable top, and a secure wrist closure.

Shoes For most young riders, a pair of cycling-specific shoes are an unnecessary expense, but for those who've shown a real love for the sport, the performance enhancement offered by shoes designed for the rigors of cycling can be a big plus. For most, a mountain bike–oriented shoe—one with a soft sole that is easy to walk in—is the perfect choice. There are even a number of skateboard-inspired shoes from companies such as Vans that combine a cool look with a rigid sole.

PART II

FIRST PEDAL STROKES

Around the Block Today,
Around the World Tomorrow

"What was so awesome about being a kid and learning to ride was that first, I rode to the end of the street. Then it was round the block, and eventually, me and all my buddies would ride all over town, just discovering everything," says Discovery Channel rider Michael Barry, a racer since his early teens. "To me that's what cycling is all about. I may be a professional racer, but not a whole lot has changed since those early days. I still do it because I love riding and I love the adventure that seems to lie around every corner."

Between the time when they're infants (and your bike is most likely collecting dust in the corner) and the age of 6 or 8 years, when they're liberated from the driveway and have a thirst for the specific kind of adventure that can only be found on two wheels, your kids will grow and change so rapidly that you'll have a tough time keeping track of it. Here's a guide to the steps that most kids go through, what you should expect from them during each phase, and what you'll need to teach them.

INFANCY

Especially with your first baby, you're likely to be chomping at the bit to get out of the house with your young one. To carry their precious cargo, many parents look to trailers or even to baby seats that strap on the back of a bike. But it's not recommended, and it may even be illegal in your state, to take a child under the age of 1 out on a bike. Under 1 year of age, a baby's head composes roughly 25 percent of her bodyweight. That's two and a half times the adult ratio. The best way to get your infant out in the fresh air is the tried-and-true stroller. Because a baby can lie completely prone, a stroller helps her to support the weight of her head, something she can't do on her own at this age. Strollers for jogging or for use on wide, smooth trails are easy to find, and, because they have pneumatic tires and a smartly designed suspension sling, they are perfect for infants.

As a new parent, you may be missing the hours that you devoted to working out prior to the arrival of your little bundle of joy. While you're likely to be exhausted and a little slaphappy from the lack of sleep, it may still be a good thing to squeeze in a little exercise just to keep the blood flowing. For most new parents, the only good time to squeeze in a workout is when the baby is napping or in the evening, so the following workouts make sense.

Ride a Bike Trainer Even if it's the middle of the summer, riding a stationary bike trainer for as little as a half hour can get your heart rate going, burn off a few calories, and provide some much-needed mental relaxation. The real benefit of this workout is that you won't be away from home in the event of an emergency.

Try Yoga Whether you do it at a local studio or on your own in a quiet part of the house, yoga is a great way to maintain flexibility in muscles and tendons, stimulate bloodflow, and relax your mind. Even just 15 minutes of controlled breathing and light stretching will put your body and mind back into a healthier state.

Jump Rope Grab a high-quality jump rope—they're often made from plastic these days—and start skipping. After just a minute or two, you'll see why everyone from professional boxers to Olympic swimmers uses this form of exercise as a core part of their training.

Jumping rope builds your quads and calves, increases flexibility in your arms and shoulders, and gets your heart moving at a very high rate. The best thing about jumping rope is that it requires only a small amount of space and a $10 "rope."

THE TODDLER YEARS (AGES 1 TO 2)

By the time a child hits his first birthday, his neck and shoulder muscles should be developed enough to support the weight of the helmet and the jarring encountered in a baby seat or bicycle trailer. Between kids' seats that strap on the back of a bike and child trailers that you pull behind the bike, there are a number of options for getting your young one outside. Just don't forget that you've got a baby on board. Although your little one has made tremendous developmental strides, he is still largely undeveloped and needs to be treated with extreme care. Even in the most supportive trailer or child seat, it's important to ride on roads that are generally smooth. Every 5 miles or so, you should also stop, get off the bike, and check your child's position.

Kids' Seats These molded plastic seats work for children up to about 50 pounds, and they are designed to support a child's neck and back while protecting his legs and feet. Most have a solid four-point harness and a padded bar at the waist. The best thing about these seats is that your child sits very close to you—so close that he can touch your back and hips. The biggest downside is that, because the kid seat sits so high on the bike, it makes the ride less stable than normal. The kid seat is probably the best option for people who own two bikes, since they can mount the seat on one bike and use it exclusively for short jaunts around town.

Trailers Thanks to a sturdy design and low center of gravity, a child trailer can hold kids up to about 4 years of age, including multiple kids with a total weight of less than 100 pounds. The best trailers are sturdy, easy to tow, and nearly impossible to tip over. Another plus is that it's easy to carry all the things a toddler needs when she leaves home: sippy cups, extra diapers, layers of clothing, stuffed animals, pacifiers, bottles of milk, snacks, etc. The downside of most children's trailers is that it's tough to see what the passenger(s) are doing while you're zipping down the street. Because most trailers are roomy, it's possible that a child could crawl around inside the trailer or even stick a hand or leg outside the confines of the trailer. If you're worried about safety with a trailer, one option is to strap your child into a car seat and then strap her *and* the seat into the trailer.

2 TO 4 YEARS

Even past the terrible twos, kids love to be towed in trailers or brought along in a baby seat. It's so relaxing that they'll often fall asleep on a longer ride. But between the ages of 2 and 3, kids will also start to explore riding on their own, usually on a tricycle. By the time they hit the halfway point of their third year, many young ones will be eager to hop on a small two-wheeler outfitted with training wheels. As with every other developmental stage in your child's life, be wary of setting expectations that are fixed to a particular age. Kids will crawl, walk, run, talk, and ride when they're ready and not before.

At this age, most children have an intuitive understanding of how to pedal the bike, but they still need to develop their balance, body position, and ability to steer and stop the bike. This is a great age to make learning fun by challenging your child to steer around small rocks in the driveway or to stop before hitting a chalk line drawn across the sidewalk. The more fun and interesting you make it, the more likely she will be to want to develop her handling and balance. It's a great idea to get together with other parents and children in your neighborhood for a morning of fun riding at a local playground. Kids learn best when simply following the example of others their size.

When your child first climbs aboard a two-wheeler with training wheels, he will likely feel ready to take on the world. Oftentimes at this age, a young, unskilled rider will be tempted to try to keep up with older siblings or neighbors who are on bigger bikes and who are stronger and more skilled. More often than not, that scenario will lead to disastrous consequences. Be certain to take a few hours to help your child relearn the braking and handling of the bike and to reiterate the full range of traffic and safety rules. Also be sure to set limits as to where your young one can ride and when. It's probably a good idea to keep him in the driveway at this age, saving the round-the-block jaunts for times when one or both parents are present. As every parent knows, time flies so fast with kids that, before long, your young one will be tearing out of the driveway on Saturday morning and riding to school during the week. Use the earlier years to ease him gently into riding.

4 TO 6 YEARS

From the first days in school to taking a stab at organized sports, these years are filled with excitement and challenge. Between the ages of 4 and 6, most kids will have developed a good sense of balance, a smooth pedaling motion, and the ability to steer with relative precision.

At this age, proper braking is the most difficult challenge because most children do not have the strength and coordination to master the use of hand-actuated brakes. To help your child learn this crucial skill, it's best to show him how to squeeze both brake levers at the same time while keeping his eyes on the road or trail. Initially, it will take all the strength he can muster to simply get the brake pads to move toward the rim. As he improves, you'll need to explain to him that the front brake, which provides about 75 percent of the bike's total stopping power, is more powerful and should be used with greater care and finesse than the rear brake.

During this time frame, kids will make the transition from riding with training wheels to mastering life on two wheels. At this age, they'll most likely fit on a bike with 16-inch wheels. Another good option is to fit a "trailer bike." This is a bike with a normal rear half mated to a modified front half, which in turn attaches to the back of an adult bike, effectively making it an inline three-wheeler. On a trailer bike, a child can experience the thrill of riding on the road without the danger of balancing, steering, and braking on his own. It's also a great way for him to experience the adventure of riding beyond his neighborhood. Whether in an urban landscape or along a country road, this initial taste of freedom and adventure will fuel a rider's fire for years to come.

Another riding option for kids of this age and skill level is to put them on the back of a specially outfitted tandem bike. Thanks to kid "stoker" kits from companies such as da Vinci (www.davincitandems.com), a

(continued on page 30)

One of the most exciting and memorable days in both a child's and parent's life is when a young one rides on her own for the first time. After much trial and error, *Bicycling* magazine has developed a preferred method that is actually much different than the run-beside-the-bike method that most of us were taught. Based on experience, this method has been shown to help children learn to ride on their own in less time and with fewer spills.

Using an adjustable wrench, unbolt the training wheels from your child's bike and lower her saddle so that it is easy for her to sit on the saddle with her feet flat on the ground. While your child is saddled up and straddling the bike, it's a good time to remind her where the brakes are located, how they work, and when she'll need to apply them. It's also a great time to make sure that she is wearing the proper attire (pants with the leg cuffed to prevent it from becoming stuck in the chain) and to double-check the fit of her helmet (see page 14).

Head to a smooth, grassy field that has a gentle downslope 30 to 50 yards in length. Obviously, you'll want it to be clear of any type of vehicular traffic, but also be sure that it's not too steep, that it's wide enough to allow for unplanned weaving, and that it has grass short enough to allow the bike to roll freely. Before setting your young one off, take a few minutes to walk the hill, looking for holes, debris, or other unexpected hazards.

Once the stage is set, stand halfway up the hill and have your child straddle the bike with her feet flat on the ground while you place one hand on the handlebars and one on the back of the saddle.

After explaining to her one final time what the brakes are for, where she should try to steer, and how to fall if a spill seems inevitable, have her lift her feet a few inches off the ground (being sure not to put them on the bike's pedals). Once she's ready, give her a slight push and let the bike coast down the hill. You'll be tempted to run beside your child for safety, but because you're on a grassy field, the bike isn't likely to pick up too much speed or feel out of control. If you can't resist, be sure to run behind her so she can feel how balance works and have a sense of accomplishing this feat on her own.

Continue to have your child roll down the hill until she feels abso-

Training wheels are a great tool for your child while he masters balance and precise steering.

lutely comfortable with the sensation and doesn't waver or fall. The next step is to have her roll down the hill with her feet on the pedals, making sure to keep her pedals parallel to the ground. This should be an easy transition if she's mastered the first step, but be sure to give her plenty of runs so she can get used to the new sensation of having her feet a little higher.

Once your child feels like she's mastered coasting with her feet on the pedals, have her begin to pedal slowly as she rolls down the hill. Make sure that she's not cranking on the pedals but lightly rotating them just to feel the sensation of pedaling and balancing at the same time. You'll also be able to raise her saddle up to a height at which her leg is extended to roughly 80 percent of its overall length.

Eventually, your child will master pedaling down the grassy slope on her own—hopefully before you tire of walking up and down the hill. The next step is to take her to a paved playground or even the end of a quiet cul-de-sac for practice riding on her own. This time, encourage her to experiment with turns and quick stops. This is also a good time to give her a refresher on how to watch for traffic and other hazards while riding.

Last step? Have a cold drink and maybe a celebratory ice cream cone—it's been a big day for both of you.

child can experience real riding right behind an adult. The best thing about a kid stoker kit is that, thanks to an incredible range of adjustment, it will fit most children for years and years—certainly long after they want to be seen engaged in an activity as uncool as riding around with their parents!

6 TO 8 YEARS

At this age, most children have developed their strength, balance, and fine motor skills to the point where they are capable of using hand brakes and shifting gears. It will take plenty of time and patience on

. . . .
5 SKILLS YOUR CHILD NEEDS TO LEARN AND HOW TO TEACH THEM
. . . .

1. BE SAFE. *Before taking the first pedal stroke, every child needs to remember that safety is the most important part of riding. It's even more important than having fun because you can't have fun until you're absolutely, positively safe. Safety always starts with a helmet, appropriate clothing (including shoes), and a well-tuned bike. Once you're rolling, safety means constantly assessing the situation, constantly looking for danger, and knowing the path away from it. Tell your child: Being safe on a bike isn't a fixed goal; it's a process that never, ever comes to an end.*

2. GET GOING. *Have your child sit in a stationary position with one foot firmly planted on the ground and the other on a pedal that is pointed toward the handlebar (roughly 2 o'clock). Tell her to step hard on the pedal, bring her other foot up, and pull up slightly with the opposite hand. Tell your child: The key to a smooth start is to keep your upper body as relaxed as possible. It keeps you from swerving all over the place as you build up speed and it will keep you from tiring early.*

3. FLY STRAIGHT. *As with picking up steam, once your young rider is cranking down the block, the best thing for her to do is*

. . . .

everyone's part for them to develop the right touch with both, but at this age they should have the physical and mental capacity for the task.

Kids in this age range will leave their 12-inch-wheeled bikes sitting in the garage and upgrade to a 20-inch-wheeled bike favored by most older kids. This is also the age at which kids will be able to upgrade to a bike with suspension (front, rear, or both), knobby tires, and trail-tough components.

Whether on a 20-inch BMX bike or a suspension-equipped mountain bike, most 6- to 8-year-olds will be eager for adventure, both

· ·

to relax her upper body and let the bike's gyroscopic effect help to keep it moving forward in a direct line. Tell your child: The key to riding in a straight line is to relax and embrace the speed; don't be fearful of it. As long as you can control it, speed is your friend.

4. CORNER WITH EASE. *Now that your child can get going and ride in a straight line, it's time for her to learn how to take a corner. The best strategy is for her to relax her upper body, slow slightly before entering the corner, and lean the bike slightly while turning the handlebars in the direction she wants to go. Tell your child: The key to cornering smoothly and quickly is to shave off speed before you enter the corner. Once you're turning the bike, you should be able to take pressure off the brakes completely.*

5. STOP! *No repertory of riding skills would be complete without the final step—stopping. The best way to shave off speed is to squeeze both brake levers firmly and smoothly, not with one great pump. Applying supple pressure will prevent the wheels from locking up and making her lose control. Tell your child: The front brake generates roughly 75 percent of the bike's total stopping power. Panicking and squeezing the front stopper too hard can result in an "endo"—ejection over the handlebars.*

· ·

on- and off-road. If you've taught your kids well up to this point, it should be no problem for them to adapt to riding off-road and outside the playground. Riding off-road is a great skill and confidence-builder for a young rider. It's more fun, more challenging, and, without any vehicular traffic around, actually safer than riding on the street.

Thanks to their physical development and an added measure of freedom, your young ones will be taking longer rides than ever. Here are a few things they'll need to consider if they want to enjoy every minute.

Drink Water For every hour that your child is riding, he should drink at least half of a 16-ounce water bottle—more on hot days. For really big adventures, a hydration pack such as those made by Camelbak is a necessity that no good rider would be without.

Wear Sunscreen Just like adults, children should wear a minimum of SPF 15 sunscreen every time they ride—even if it doesn't seem sunny. A sport-specific sunscreen, which will not block the skin's pores, is the most effective type. For cycling, be careful to apply a heavy coat to the tops of your child's ears and to his face, forehead, neck, arms, and hands.

Dress Right Whether he tells you or not, most often, looking cool for his friends is more important than anything else where wardrobe is concerned. Yet, the longer he's on a bike, the more he needs truly protective gear that will stay dry and comfortable when he pedals. This includes a helmet, gloves, sturdy shoes, a shirt made from a wicking fabric such as polyester or wool, and pants that are loose-fitting without being baggy and that don't have thick seams that will chafe his legs or backside.

PART III

···

YOUR CHILD AT 8 TO 12 YEARS OLD

Fun, Challenge, Comfort, and Control:
Key Concepts for the Budding Cyclist

···

WHY CYCLING MATTERS NOW

Think back to when you were 8 years old. It's probably safe to say that, as a third-grader, you were more concerned with quality playground time than you were with honing lifelong skills in any particular sport. And you turned out okay, right? Keep that in mind when it comes to cycling with your preteen child—he probably isn't thinking about becoming a lifelong cyclist. He's probably thinking that he wants to have fun, usually with his friends, while riding around. "It's great to have a plan and a goal and everything, but if you're not focused on having fun, riding a bicycle can be drudgery," says Canadian Michael Barry of the Discovery Channel Team. At this point, it's simply your job to give your child the tools to do that safely, and to introduce her to the rules of the road. If you happen to be going to a cycling event, though—whether as a racer or a spectator—be sure to take your child along. It's the best way to show that a bike can be fun for more than just a lap around the block with her pals.

Cycling parents, rejoice! These are the years when your child develops the necessary cognitive functions (read: judgment) to start riding on the road, with traffic. Still, don't take your child for a spin on a busy road on his 8th birthday. Introduce him to the rules of the road (see page 4) gradually, as you slowly broaden his riding horizons from neighborhood jaunts to honest-to-goodness rides.

....

Truth be told, kids need to be inspired to ride their bicycles now more than ever. According to the American Obesity Association (AOA), more than 15 percent of American children (ages 6 through 19) are obese—a percentage that has increased dramatically over the last 10 years. Being so overweight at such a young age sets the stage for a host of maladies later in life, including diabetes, high blood pressure, and heart disease. The AOA fact sheet titled "Obesity in Youth" says it best: "Overweight during childhood and particularly adolescence is related to increased morbidity and mortality in later life." Sounds

The American Obesity Association says that more than 15 percent of American children are obese. Regular exercise like cycling can significantly reduce your child's chance of becoming overweight.

like every parent's nightmare. But there's also an answer: physical activity. Unfortunately, our kids often aren't as active as we think.

Remember that playground time you so eagerly anticipated when you were in third grade? These days, playground time is disappearing. And so are physical education classes. According to the Centers for Disease Control and Prevention (CDC), during the 1990s, the percentage of schools offering PE programs dropped from 40 percent to 25 percent, meaning that many kids in the United States aren't learning about the lifelong benefits of physical exercise. What's worse, researchers found that the resulting decrease in activity led to unwanted weight gain in the inactive students.

This is where parents—and bikes—can make a difference. We all know that riding a bike is fun and liberating, but making bikes an everyday part of your child's world could also save her health later in life. Keep in mind, though, that cycling for better health is an argument that only a parent can love. Kids aren't going to be very receptive to it. They just want to have fun. The key to opening their eyes to the benefits of riding is to keep it light and easy. Read on to learn the ins and outs of keeping cycling fun, interesting, safe, and exciting for your preteen.

EQUIPMENT: KEEPING PACE WITH A CHANGING BODY

This time in a child's life can be summed up with one word: *puberty*. It tends to strike sometime in the 8- to 12-year-old time frame, and it sticks around for anywhere from 2 to 7 years. And, as we all know, the only constant during puberty is change; this period of rapid maturation is marked by growth spurts, emotional stress, and, of course, sexual development.

The biggest challenge for you as far as your child and cycling goes? Growth. This is the time when your child will transition from riding a smaller-wheeled kid's bike to a more adult-sized ride. His developing body and increased ability to ride for longer distances and at greater speed mean that he'll be able to use—and in some instances, he'll require—more advanced cycling clothing such as cycling shoes, clipless pedals, padded cycling shorts, and even knee and elbow pads. When he's first starting out, though, it's unlikely that your child needs

Make sure your child wears a Consumer Product Safety Commission–certified helmet on every ride.

a closet full of cycling-specific gear. Instead, as with the other aspects of your child's burgeoning love of cycling, now is the time to focus on the basics.

THE HELMET

There's only one piece of cycling gear that's absolutely mandatory, from the minute you first introduce your child to a bicycle: a helmet. Proper-fitting helmets that have been certified by the Consumer Product Safety Commission (CPSC) could prevent 85 percent of cyclists' head injuries. And there's good news: You don't need to buy a super-expensive helmet to protect your child's noggin—some CPSC–certified helmets cost as little as $20. And, thanks to modern materials and construction techniques, inexpensive helmets are nearly as light and comfortable as the lids that Tour de France winners wear.

SHORTS

Other than a helmet, no piece of clothing can improve the riding experience as much as cycling-specific shorts. Let's be straight here, though: At this age, cycling-specific shorts aren't a necessity—in fact, your child will likely feel less conspicuous heading out the door in casual clothes. These shorts will become more appealing as your young rider starts to spend more time in the saddle. Cycling shorts are less likely to snag on the bike's seat than a regular pair of shorts (adding to your child's safety when she's trying to maneuver on and off the saddle); the pad in the crotch, called a chamois, helps reduce pressure, irritation, and chafing (see "Why Is It Called a Chamois?" on page 38); and, as a bonus, the material dries quickly, for added comfort.

Sizing Up Shorts

Quality shorts don't need to be expensive. At this age, that's a good thing, as your child will likely outgrow the shorts before they wear out. Still, there are a few features to look for to help you choose the right pair.

Snug, But Not Tight Traditional cycling shorts are meant to be form-fitting. If the shorts aren't snug, the fabric will be loose in all the wrong spots (such as in the crotch), making it easy to get snagged on the bike's seat. The best-fitting shorts will be comfortably snug, and they shouldn't pinch anywhere. If the shorts are uncomfortable, especially around the waist or at the leg openings, try on another pair.

Chamois Size A thick chamois likely isn't necessary. All your child needs is something thick enough to protect her from any seams in the shorts and provide a little extra padding. If the pad is *so* dense that it feels like a diaper, it'll be less comfortable than even a pair of jeans. One key fact: You don't wear underwear with cycling shorts—the seams will only cause chafing and irritation.

Go Baggy It's true: Baggy cycling shorts (often favored by mountain bikers) are a viable and often favored alternative to traditional cycling shorts. If your child is spending a lot of time in the saddle but she balks at tight Lycra, baggies are a great choice. Since most baggy shorts come with a snug-fitting liner, much of the same shorts selection advice still applies. When your child is trying out a set of baggy shorts, make sure that they *aren't* baggy where it counts; they should fit close to the crotch so that they don't get caught on the bike's saddle.

··
WHY IS IT CALLED A CHAMOIS?
··

Look up the word *chamois* (pronounced *shammy*) in the dictionary, and you'll see that the word means "a small, goatlike antelope found in the mountains of southern Europe." So why is the pad in cycling shorts called a chamois? When chamois pads were first used in cycling shorts back in the early 1900s, they were made of leather—in particular, chamois leather. Real chamois pads were used until the early 1990s, when they were phased out in favor of today's synthetic materials, which are more efficient at moving moisture away from the skin, easy to care for, and incredibly durable.

··

GLOVES

This is about more than protection. Sure, a glove will protect a child's palms from getting scraped up in a fall (and that alone is worth the price, which can be as little as $10 for a basic pair), but a good-fitting pair of gloves can also improve grip—meaning a stronger connection to the handlebar—and dampen vibrations, lessening hand fatigue so that your child's fingers can easily give the brake lever a hard, fast squeeze at any time.

JERSEY

A cycling-specific jersey is even further down the list of necessities—your child isn't putting in the miles required to reap the benefits of high-tech, sweat-wicking fabrics and full-length zippers for ventilation. But if he does a considerable amount of riding, or complains that his T-shirt makes him feel cold or clammy, it's likely time to pony up for a jersey. When it comes to this purchase, let your child be your guide—he'll be able to tell you whether he prefers a form-fitting or a baggy jersey, or one that's more subdued versus one that's covered with bright logos. After all, if your child doesn't like it, he won't wear it.

SHOES

Simply put, your child's cycling shoes should match his skill level. Early on, sneakers will be enough—just make sure that the laces are out of the way (tucked in, or tied off to the side) so that they don't get caught in the drivetrain. But as your child's skills progress to the point that he's obviously interested in a specific area of cycling, you'll likely want to introduce him to clipless pedals (if he's into road riding or cross-country mountain biking) or flat BMX-style pedals (if he's into BMX racing, dirt jumping, or freeriding).

Time to shop for bike shoes? Keep these tips in mind.

Fit For BMX-style flat pedals, you want a close-fitting shoe with flat, grippy rubber bottoms. Skateboard sneakers work well. You want a close-fitting shoe when using clipless pedals as well, so that any side-to-side movement of the foot results in movement of the shoe—that way, your child can clip out when he needs to without resorting to dramatic foot twisting. Also, don't give in to the temptation to buy bigger shoes than necessary so that your child will grow into them. If the shoes are too big, his feet won't line up properly, which sets the stage for knee injuries and poor pedaling form.

Stiffness A stiffer sole makes for more efficient power transfer while pedaling. However, stiff-soled shoes—especially plastic-bottomed road shoes—can be difficult to walk in. For a young clipless-pedal rider, medium-stiffness shoes with rubber treads offer the best compromise of stiffness and walkability.

THE RIGHT BIKE FOR YOUR CHILD

Where gear is concerned, there's never been a better time to be a cyclist. Advances in technology and manufacturing (not to mention an increased interest in cycling in general, thanks to Lance Armstrong's unprecedented 7-year domination of the Tour de France and the continued strength of the Discovery Channel Pro Cycling Team) mean that today's bikes are less expensive and better made than those on the market even 5 years ago.

But there's a downside to this, too. If you've been in the bike aisle of a department store recently, let alone in a bike shop, you know what the potential problem is: There are so many choices out there that selecting the right bike is far from easy—especially if you don't have any guidelines to follow other than the style of bike and color your child likes. At this age, she's stepping beyond the first bike—likely a smaller-wheeled bike with a coaster brake—and into the realm of larger bikes that are incredibly similar to adult bicycles. Don't fall into the "this bike looks nice, let's get it" trap. Though it's important that your child loves the look of her new bike, the same rule applies both to children's and adult bikes: Fit comes first.

Youth bicycles are measured according to wheel size; chances are, your child is tall enough and coordinated enough that you're looking at something with 20- or 24-inch wheels. (Generally speaking, 20-inch-wheeled bikes fit most 6- to 9-year-olds; 24-inch-wheeled bikes fit most kids 9 and up.) How do you know when your child is ready to move up in size? Watch her ride. If the seat is raised and she still

BIKE SHOP VS. BIG BOX

There's only one area where a department store wins out over a bike shop, and that's price. But when you're purchasing a bike for your child, the bottom line is about more than just dollars. It's about safety and reliability. One basic rule to follow: The more a kids' bike is like an adult bike, the better it is. A bike that has quick-release wheels and handlebar-mounted shifters is almost certainly better than one without.

Think about it: Not only do bike shop employees specialize solely in bicycles, but many are also dedicated cyclists—meaning that if you walk through the door with a general idea of what you're looking for and what you want to spend, they'll immediately be able to help you narrow your choices. And after that, they'll work with you closely to make sure that the bike you choose fits your child like a glove, and they'll tell you how to spot when your child is outgrowing the bike. Plus, you can rest assured knowing that the bike was professionally assembled; most shops stand behind their bikes and assembly to the point that they offer free tune-ups and service for a year after purchase.

You're not likely to find such customer service at a big-box store.

seems hunched over and her legs seem cramped on the bike, it's time for a new ride. What you're looking for beyond that depends on the type of riding you and your child will be doing together, and the distances you hope to cover.

THE HYBRID

This is easily the most popular bike style for growing riders; though it looks like a mountain bike, it's designed to be used both on-road and off—exactly the mix of riding that most kids this age are going to do. It's perfect for short family rides, trips to the playground, or traveling to school. It's not a speedster, nor is it designed for BMX-style jumping or tricks. If straight road performance or dirt-jump prowess is what your child wants, check out "Road Bikes," page 45, or "BMX Bikes," page 46.

At this size and price range, frames are generally made of lighter-

- -

Rare is the department-store employee trained in the intricacies of bike fit, meaning there's a good chance you'll get a bike that's too big (or too small). Be wary of being told that your child will "grow into" a bike when the truth is that if it doesn't fit, it will be difficult to control, making learning tough. Plus, as department store employees aren't professional bike mechanics, you won't know for sure that bikes purchased from a megastore have been properly assembled. Is that something you want to think about the first time your child heads out on her new bike? Probably not.

The other part of the bike-buying equation is that most kids outgrow their two-wheelers before they wear out. If you're hoping to save some money but don't want to purchase a bike from a department store, visit some local yard sales. (Though buying a used bike online might seem like a good idea, there's no way to guarantee a good fit without seeing a bike in person so that your child can try it out.) Of course, this option only works if you know about bike fit and how to spot a quality bike. Fortunately, if you use this chapter as a guide, you'll be able to do both.

- -

weight aluminum, though there are a few quality steel kids' bike frames. (If you're in the market for a higher-end hybrid, many companies make high-performance versions that are as light and nimble as a standard road bike but have a more back-friendly position.) The bottom line? Don't be put off by (or sold on) what kind of material is used to make the frame. Instead, judge the overall quality of the bike's construction by checking out the following components.

Wheels Steel rims are a warning sign; look for light aluminum rims (which will never be chrome-plated) with individual spokes and spoke nipples so the wheel can be trued (straightened) should your child hit something a little too hard. Not only are aluminum rims lighter than steel, but they also provide a better braking surface—definitely important as your child transitions from pedal-based coaster brakes to hand-operated brake levers. Also, check that the wheels are held on with quick-release levers—another sign of a quality bike—instead of being bolted in place.

Suspension Suspension is far from mandatory for bikes at this size. However, if you plan to take your child with you out on the local trails, it could be worth the premium in price (as much as double that of a similar bike with no suspension). Only the highest-priced suspension bikes offer the quality construction and adjustments necessary to make the suspension pieces work properly. If you can't change the spring rate, or adjust the rebound damping (which controls the rate at which the suspension returns to the normal position after it hits a bump), you could end up with a fork that doesn't move at all or that moves too much when your child hits a bump, or with a rear suspension that acts like a bucking bronco with every hit. Look for, and ask how to use, the adjustments if you decide that a suspension bike is right for your child.

Gears Now is the time to introduce the concept of shifting—if you haven't done so already. Most bikes in this size range come with 21 speeds, which means that there are a seven-gear cassette on the rear wheel and three chainrings on the crankset. (Some bikes have a variation on this theme; for example, a seven-gear cassette with a single chainring on the crankset, which is protected by a bashguard.)

Thanks to a wider range of gears, 21-speed bikes are the most well-rounded, and they make the perfect choice for growing cyclists.

Derailleurs and Shifters If the bike has multiple gears—and it should, unless it's a true BMX bike—it will have derailleurs and shifters. You have two brand options here: Shimano and SRAM. Performance between the two is almost identical. The difference lies in the way the shifters work: To shift with SRAM's Grip Shift shifter, you twist the grip; with Shimano's RapidFire shifter, you use your thumb and forefinger to move a shift lever. Beware of bikes that don't have shifters and derailleurs from one of these two companies—their absence can be indicative of other shortcomings in the bike's construction and equipment. For example, cheaply made frames use a thin, stamped rear derailleur mount that's likely to bend and flex when your child tries to shift, meaning that changing gears will be iffy at best. Very often, these frames won't carry a Shimano or SRAM rear derailleur.

Brakes Say good-bye to the coaster brake; this bike will come with hand-operated brake levers. Most are what's known as "linear pull" or "direct pull" rim brakes. Cables run from the brake levers at the handlebar to brakes mounted on the fork at the front and rear of the bike. The brakes have long arms; when you pull the brake lever, a cable pulls the arms together and the brake pad squeezes the rim, slowing the bike.

Just like your car, some hardcore-use mountain bikes at this size come with disc brakes, which are safer, stronger, and more dependable than rim brakes. Pads situated closer to the center of the wheel clamp onto a metal disc attached to the wheel's hub when the brake lever is squeezed, slowing the bike. Unless your child is doing serious trail or stunt riding, disc brakes aren't necessary and simply add cost and complexity to your child's bike.

Bearings These allow parts of the bike to rotate smoothly and freely, with little friction. Look for serviceable ball bearings (meaning they can be adjusted and greased) on all moving parts: the hubs, pedals, bottom bracket, and headset. They can be tough to see, so there's a quick way to judge the overall bearing quality of a bike: the pedals.

They should feel almost fluid when you turn them; if there is any sense of grit, or if it looks as though the pedals are simply a piece of plastic skewered by a metal rod, move on.

How It Fits Standover clearance is the first fit factor to consider. Have your child swing a leg over the bike and stand, flat footed, with the top tube between his legs and the nose of the saddle almost touching his back. There should be 2 to 3 inches of clearance between his crotch and the top tube.

Since most kids' bikes have relatively steep-sloping top tubes, clearance often isn't a problem—which means it shouldn't be the sole factor in judging a bike's fit. If the bike passes the clearance test, the next step is for your child to take a test drive while you pay particular attention to the extension of his legs and arms.

To find a starting point for the seat's height, have your child stand next to the bike; use the bolt or quick-release lever on the seatpost to set the seat close to crotch height. Then have your child climb aboard

. . . .

THE ONCE-OVER

. . . .

Want to quickly assess whether a bike is worth the money? Look at these five pieces first.

1. FRAME. *Aluminum is usually better than steel; it's lighter and more nimble.*
2. WHEELS. *Aluminum wheels, individual spokes and nipples, and quick-release levers that solidly hold the wheel into the frame are a must.*
3. BRAKES. *Give the levers a squeeze—both the front and rear brakes should feel solid and be easy to activate.*
4. SHIFTERS/DERAILLEURS. *Check for a Shimano label, and run through the gears. Shifts should be quick and precise.*
5. SEATPOST. *Look for a quick-release lever that clamps tightly. When the quick release is open, the seatpost should slide up and down easily.*

. . . .

and take a spin. If his knees are uncomfortably high at the top of the pedal stroke, raise the seat; if he's struggling to reach the pedals at the bottom of the stroke, lower the seat. You want to reach a happy medium—he should be getting good leg extension without overextending (there should be a slight bend in his knee at the bottom of the pedal stroke), and he shouldn't feel that he's too high in the air. If you can't find the balance between being cramped and overextending, opt for a saddle height that is slightly lower, as there's less negative effect on the bike's handling and a lower chance of injury.

With the seat set to the correct height, the final adjustment should be handlebar height and extension. When the position is correct, your child should be able to ride with his upper body at no less than a 45-degree angle—bend forward any farther and he'll be too stretched out to control the bike properly. Raise or lower the handlebar and stem until you find the right spot. Check the fit by having him practice a few left- and right-hand turns, as well as some quick stops. When properly positioned, he should be able to do so easily, safely, and comfortably.

NICHE BIKES

So you say the cycling bug has bitten your child—he's talking incessantly about Lance Armstrong or Matt Hoffman and has taken a clear interest in a specific cycling niche, such as BMX, dirt jumping, or road racing? Not to worry, there are high-quality bikes to match your child's interest . . . and size. Many of the same attributes of the general-purpose bike still apply, with a few notable exceptions.

Road Bikes

Drop-bar road bikes are relatively uncommon in children's sizes, but with the recent success of Lance Armstrong, they have become more popular. Be aware that fit is much more specific on a road bike. Along with proper leg extension (meaning that your child's leg only has a slight bend at the bottom of the pedal stroke), reach is extremely important. Check your child's position three ways: when she's riding with her hands on the top of the handlebar, with her hands on the brake hoods, and with them in the drops. It's okay for her upper body to be bent at slightly more than 45 degrees on a road bike, but she shouldn't be so stretched out in any one position that she's uncomfortable or lacks proper control. Also, double-check that she can easily and quickly reach the brake levers when riding in the drops.

BMX Bikes

BMX racing bikes (often made of aluminum so they're lighter for racing) and BMX freestyle bikes (often made of steel so that they can withstand lots of abuse) are the most fun to ride and stand up to an incredible amount of abuse, even if they aren't as versatile as their general-purpose brethren. These bikes have only one gear, and some have only a single brake. They don't have any suspension. BMX racing bikes and dirt-jumping bikes most often have 20-inch wheels. As with road bikes, the key difference between BMX bikes and general-purpose bikes is fit—there is only one standard BMX frame size, and it's meant to fit all riders, young and old. Though smaller children will have no problem comfortably pedaling a BMX bike while seated, as your child gets older, he's more likely to feel cramped on the bike. That's because BMX bikes are meant to be ridden for short, fast bursts, mostly while standing.

SKILLS: LIFE LESSONS

To date, your child's time on a bike has likely revolved around less-than-serious outings—a trip to a friend's house, maybe a ride around the neighborhood. And, any time he wanted to tackle something more—and any time there was any amount of traffic around—you did what any responsible parent would: You went along for the ride to make sure that he was safe, while he focused on having fun. That's what parents are for—and that's what kids do.

It's important to keep that in mind as you enter the next stage of your child's cycling life—the stage marked by the appearance of a bike with multiple gears and hand-operated brakes, which any young rider needs to learn how to use effectively. Remember that while your child is maturing and his ability to make complex-yet-quick decisions is increasing, he still just wants to have fun. Nothing will turn a kid off faster than making every bike ride a lesson or skill-building session. Still, it's every bike-conscious parent's responsibility to teach their children the skills they need to be safe on the bike, as well as to squeeze every ounce of fun out of their rides.

As with the rest of life, it all starts with the basics.

Tip: Avoid wobbly starts. When your child is starting from a standstill, have him begin with one pedal pointing toward the handlebar. This will let him get a quick, solid pedal stroke in, so that he can get the bike moving and have enough time to put a foot on the other pedal.

SHIFTING AND BRAKING

Our hands are responsible for much of our comfort and safety while we ride. They work the shifters to change gears so that our legs can work at the right pace while we climb or descend; and they squeeze the brake levers that scrub speed so that we stay in control. It's a huge jump to go from a bike with no gears and a coaster brake to a bike with front and rear brakes and a range of gears. It takes time to learn to use them properly; fortunately, the learning process can be fun for both you and your child.

Shifting Simplicity

Look at the shifters on your child's bike—they should display numbers depending on the bike's number of gears: likely 1 through 3 on the left-hand shifter (which works the front derailleur) and 1 through 7 (if it's a 21-speed bike), or a similar range of numbers, on the right-hand shifter. These numbers are how you want to introduce your child to gears—avoid using confusing terms like "chainrings" or "cogs" when you talk about shifting. Besides, watching the chainring or cogs requires that your child not watch where she's going—not a good idea.

As a rule, lower numbers make pedaling easier and are good for going slower. Higher numbers make pedaling harder and are good for going faster. Don't mix extreme high and low numbers—no 1 front, 7 rear or 3/1 combinations—because they are less efficient and could result in a major drivetrain failure. Have your young rider shift around anywhere in between to make herself comfortable.

Once your child understands these basic operational techniques, it's time to ride! Go to a playground, driveway, or stretch of traffic-free road, and ride some loops with your child. Have her get used to the feel of shifting as she rides—into harder gears as she goes downhill, into easier gears as she climbs or before stopping. Gently remind her to shift if you see her struggling to push a big gear or spinning out.

Tip: Keep it short. Don't talk about a skill for more than 3 minutes before you put the skill into practice; and don't do any specific skill drill for more than 10 minutes at a time. Any more than that, and your child will get bored or frustrated. Practice for a few minutes, then go for a ride. You'll both have more fun . . . and your child can continue to practice outside of a "lesson" format.

Braking Basics

Brakes are incredibly easy to understand: The left lever works the front brake; the right lever works the rear. Make sure the levers are set where your child can easily reach them: When she's seated on the bike with her hands on the handlebar, the brake levers should be in reach if she stretches out her fingers. She shouldn't need to bend her wrist awkwardly or stretch uncomfortably to reach the brakes.

The lesson: Squeezing both brakes simultaneously will quickly stop the bike. But too much front brake can flip your child over or cause her to lose control of the bike, while too much rear brake will lock up the rear wheel, causing the bike to slide. When teaching your child how to stop quickly, have her stand on the pedals and shift her weight backward on the bike, applying a little pressure to the front brake and a lot of pressure to the rear. For long, gentle stops, she can use the rear brake alone—though she shouldn't brake so hard that she slides.

In practice: Go to the same playground, driveway, or stretch of traffic-free road, draw a line partway down the hill (sidewalk chalk works great), and have your child practice riding to the line and stopping with her front tire as close to it as possible. Aside from building basic braking skills, this also helps her judge distances, so she can learn how long it takes to stop. Have her practice braking using just the rear brake, as well. After a few tries, take turns riding to the line and stopping—leading by example is always the best way to demonstrate a skill, and you can make it a competition. Ride at normal speed (which will be faster—and thus more challenging—for you) and see who can get closest to the line when stopping, without skidding.

THE RULES OF THE ROAD

Once your child has mastered the basics of shifting and braking, he's ready to tackle the next challenge: riding on the road, with (light) traffic. To do so safely, though, he first needs to know, and follow, the rules.

A bicycle—even a child's bicycle—is much more than a toy, and nowhere is this more evident than when riding on the road. On the road, a cyclist is expected to act in a predictable manner and obey the same traffic rules that cars must obey. In fact, this could be the easiest reminder to tell your child: "Act like a car, but remember that *cars can't see you.*"

Some key safety tips to remember include:

- Ride on the right-hand side of the road, with traffic. If you're riding in traffic with a group, always ride in single file.

- Obey all traffic signs, lights, and road markings.

- Signal when turning or stopping. To turn left, extend your left arm in the direction of the turn, parallel to the road. To turn right, either extend your right arm in the direction of the turn, parallel to the road, or extend your left arm out, parallel to the road, and bend your arm at the elbow so that your hand points upward. To signal a stop, extend your left arm out, parallel to the road, and bend at the elbow so that your hand points back and downward.

- Give the right of way to pedestrians.

- Turn from the turn lane. Always check behind you for traffic before turning into a left-hand turn lane; signal a left turn into the turn lane; and signal again for your left-hand turn.

How to Teach the Rules

Children tend to follow their parents' example, so hopefully you've been following the rules of the road (no blowing stop signs or turning without signaling) all along, on each ride with your child. Either way, when you feel that your child is mature enough to handle a solo ride with traffic, talk to her before your next ride together about being a responsible rider. Make her feel good about the lesson—she's developed enough maturity to take the next step, and that's a big deal.

Then, let her lead you on a ride along a quiet road, where you'll be able to pull alongside and chat, as well as drop behind and let her make her own decisions. Discuss signals, traffic signs, anything that comes up—and make sure you always lead by example.

ADVANCED SKILLS: BUILDING BALANCE, COACHING CORNERING

So, your child has taken to cycling like a fish to water, and you're looking for a way to improve his skills and (though you hate to admit it) still keep him close to home. Some simple orange cones can add some fun and complexity to driveway cruises. Or you can take inspiration from the freeride mountain biking crowd and build a driveway and yard-specific stunt—near ground level, of course—which can improve your child's handling skills and boost his courage, to boot.

The Balance Beam Lay a 10-foot 2 × 6 or 2 × 8 flat on a grassy surface. Have your child practice tugging on the handlebars and giving the pedals a quick stab as he leans back slightly and lofts the front tire onto the board. (The piece of wood isn't thick enough to cause any problems if your child misjudges the lift.) Then, have him ride slowly for the length of the board—the goal is to stay on top of the board for its entire length and then ride off the other end. As this gets easier, swap to a narrower piece of wood and keep practicing, or put another board at the end of this one, so he has to balance for 20 feet instead of 10.

Enjoy cycling as a family now and your child will want to ride with you in the future.

Cone Cornering Generally speaking, cornering requires that you lean the bike over a bit—a concept that your child might not be comfortable with. To help him practice, set up a line of four or five safety cones (or other, similar-sized objects), spaced about 8 feet apart. Have him practice weaving through the cones, turning left and right around them without hitting them. As your child's skill improves, encourage him to go through faster. Or move the cones out of a straight line—move the first to the left, the second to the right, and so on—so that he has to turn more to get around each cone.

Want your child to care for his own bike? Make sure he has access to the following tools whenever he feels he needs them—or, better yet, buy him his own.

FLOOR PUMP A pump with a simple gauge is best, and you can find one for less than $20. Make sure that your child knows how to read the pressure gauge—if it makes things easier, use a piece of tape to mark the gauge at the proper pressure, and have your child inflate the tires until the needle reaches the tape.

LUBE AND A RAG The important lessons here: A lubed chain runs better than a dry chain, but too much lube attracts dirt. Once a week or so (depending on how often your child rides), drip a light coating of oil on the chain, let it sit, and then wipe off the excess with a rag.

BUCKET Put a sponge or brush and a small container of dish soap in the bucket. Instant bike-cleaning kit.

THE WASH AND LUBE Though every cyclist has a unique spin on how to clean a bike, now isn't the time to inundate your child with the multitude of cleaners and sprays on the market today. This is about the basics: a hose, a bucket of soapy water, and a sponge or brush. Don't set a schedule for how often your child should clean her bike, either. Let her decide when it's dirty enough to need a washing, and let her handle the cleaning on her own.

THE PREP Sure, it's great if you have a workstand, but you don't need to use one. You can do just as well by leaning your bike against a tree.

MAINTENANCE: THE PRICE OF OWNERSHIP

Most cyclists (excluding the grease monkeys out there, of course) don't dream about bike maintenance. Simply put, we'd rather be riding than wrenching. But basic maintenance is not just something you should do, it's something you might have to do if you're stuck by the side of the road or trail with a breakdown.

Use the hose to rinse off the bike. Rule number one: Never use the hose's highest pressure on any part of the bike—you could force water into places it shouldn't be. Think "light mist," not "downpour."

THE WASH Start at the front of the bike, at the top. Grab your soapy sponge and swipe down the handlebars, front end, and fork. Dunk and squeeze out the sponge, then wash the top tube of the bike, the seat, and the rest of the front triangle. Dunk the sponge again, and wash the rear of the bike.

THE FLIP If you don't have a workstand, flip the bike over so that it's resting on the handlebars and seat. Wash the wheels, the underside of the frame, and the crankarms, chain, and chainrings. (Hint: You can clean the chain and the chainrings quickly by holding the sponge against the chainrings while you turn the pedals.)

THE RINSE Like the prep, but in reverse. Use the hose to mist the entire bike with water; flip the bike over again and rinse it off completely. Bounce the rear of the bike off the ground a few times (hold the handlebar steady with one hand, grab the bike just under the seat, raise the back end 2 or 3 inches off the ground, and drop the back end) to shake off excess water. Let the bike dry.

THE LUBE Once the bike is dry, lightly lube the chain—a small drop of lube on each link is enough. Then, wipe off any excess lube with a clean rag. Hold the rag around the chain, and use your hand to pedal backward and let the chain slide through the rag. Do a quick four-point check (see page 54), and go for a ride.

Maintenance is all part of being a responsible cyclist, and such responsibility is a great life lesson for your child. By teaching her how to maintain her own bicycle, she'll learn that a perfectly functioning bike isn't something to take for granted. Plus, she'll have a better understanding of how a bike and all its various parts work together to provide the fun of riding.

Preventive maintenance is the best. Wash your bikes every now and then, clean and lube chains, adjust derailleurs, change brake pads, keep tires inflated. A few minutes of preventive work—even if it's just a quick preride inspection—can nip major problems in the bud and eliminate a frustrating breakdown. And, if your bike isn't off being repaired, you're free to ride it. Not a bad deal.

What follows are a few introductory bike-care tips that are perfect for your preteen child. Not only are they easy to learn, but they'll also have an immediate impact on the quality—and safety—of your child's ride.

THE FOUR-POINT CHECKLIST

Teach your child to check these four areas of her bike, top to bottom, before every ride; if something seems wrong and she can't figure it out, she should come and ask you for help.

Brakes Give the brakes a quick squeeze. The levers should move freely, and they should pop back when you let go of the lever. You shouldn't be able to pull them all the way to the handlebar, either.

Saddle Check that the seat is straight and set at the right height—your young rider should be able to reach the pedals comfortably. Make sure the seatpost is held tightly in the frame. If the seatpost binder has a quick release, it should leave a slight indentation in your palm when you close it.

Wheel Quick Releases Check that the quick releases holding the wheels onto the frame are snug.

Tires Check that the tires are inflated properly. Use a pump to check tire pressure, or give them a squeeze between your thumb and forefinger—the tire should feel solid, not soft. If it's soft, pump it up. Then, give the wheel a slow spin. Check the tire for cuts (especially near the rim, where a brake pad could be rubbing) or missing tread, and make sure that the brakes don't rub any part of the rim.

Basic bike maintenance is really just that easy.

PART IV

YOUR YOUNG RIDER
AT 13 TO 18 YEARS OLD

Distance, Daring, and Independence

COMING OF AGE AS A CYCLIST

Astonishing. Honestly, there's no better way to describe the changes
that occur in the 5-year span between age 13 and age 18. Sure, you've
witnessed growth spurts in your child before now, even the initial
developmental signs that hallmark the onset of puberty, but this age
is different. You're watching your child transform into an adult.

It's been said that the changes of adolescence—the remarkable rate
of growth a teenager experiences—are second only to those seen
during the first year of life. During this period, according to the
Textbook of Adolescent Medicine, adolescents achieve the final 15 to
20 percent of their adult height, gain 50 percent of their adult body
weight, and accumulate up to 40 percent of their adult skeletal mass.
And that doesn't even take into account the strength gains that adolescents—both male and female—experience as they grow. Or the
emotional and mental development. To say that the period of adolescence will impact a child's cycling is an understatement. The truth is,

the overall growth your children experience in these years will completely change their abilities as cyclists—and hopefully solidify their love of cycling into a lifelong passion.

BEYOND FUN—CYCLING FOR LIFE

Your child's burgeoning maturity and interest in his developing body mean that he's ready to hear about the health benefits of cycling. It's time to emphasize that riding a bike is more than fun—it's adventure that's good for you.

Adolescents are obviously interested in their appearance; regular riding spurs muscle development and helps control weight. Current exercise guidelines for teenagers (and adults) are to get at least 30 minutes of exercise every day; cycling is a great way to get that exercise, not only because it's fun but also because it's a relatively low-impact sport (unlike running), so it won't cause the joint stress that can lead to injuries, especially in developing bodies.

Supporting your child's passion for cycling also puts him ahead of the curve. Currently, only about two-thirds of males and one-half of females get the recommended amount of physical activity each day. In addition, many adolescents become even less active as they approach adulthood, especially after they earn their driver's licenses. But with cycling, your child has a lifelong, personal sport in which he can experience success on his own terms. He can choose to race, or not to race; to ride with a group, or on his own; to ride the road, trail, or track. The choice is his, and that makes cycling special. It's up to you to allow him to make those choices—and to convey your own passion for cycling simply by riding and by having fun with whatever type of riding your child chooses.

THE GROUP RIDE

Teenagers and bikes were meant for each other. Teenagers have an abundance of energy, which bikes help them burn off healthfully. And bikes can give a teenager a sense of independence (especially before the appearance of a driver's license) as well as a chance to socialize with other teens. Bikes mean freedom, and that can be hard for parents—it can be tough to accept that your teen will be doing serious rides without you.

So what's a parent to do, other than trust that your child will remember the early lessons in cycling (the rules of the road, basic helmet safety, etc.)? For starters, encourage him to go on a group ride organized by a local shop, or to join a club. Organized rides are a great way for your teenager to feel some independence, socialize with other riders, and still be influenced by other responsible cyclists. It might take a few tries before you find the right environment (a club or shop ride with teenage riders), but don't let your child give up. When a group clicks, it's magic.

CHALLENGING YOUR TEEN CYCLIST

Setting—and reaching—goals is an important part of life and of being a cyclist. Too often, however, the idea of setting a cycling goal is misconstrued as "training for a race." While racing is certainly a cornerstone of the sport, it clearly is not for everybody. "We sit down at the beginning of the season with the Discovery Channel Team's directors and create a list of goals and objectives," says Discovery Channel Team rider Michael Barry. "A lot of the time, the goals aren't about winning races, they're about getting better as a rider." That's yet another key to cycling's greatness: You don't need to race to be a cyclist. You just need to ride—and there are plenty of great rides out there worthy of making a goal.

As your teen develops an interest in a specialized area of cycling— mountain biking, road riding, or something else altogether—introduce her to events that cater to her particular passions. Show her that cycling can be competitive *or* simply be a varied group of dedicated bikers riding with a single purpose. Whatever it is, it should be fun. Here are a few places to start.

NONCOMPETITIVE ROAD RIDES

Both local and national charity organizations often put together rides as fundraisers: Participants gather donations as entry fees for the rides. The rides are hugely popular, and distances often vary from relatively short (25 miles or less) to incredibly long (100+ miles). Two nationwide options: the MS150, organized by the National Multiple Sclerosis Society (www.nationalmssociety.org), and The Tour de Cure, organized by the American Diabetes Association (www.tour.diabetes.org).

"I started riding when I was 2 and racing when I was 5.

"When I got to high school we had to read the book *In the Skin of a Lion* [a novel that tells a story of the immigrants who built Toronto] and there are all these ethnic areas around my hometown of Toronto. I was so excited because I knew all the areas from having ridden around town so much. For me it was like I had seen them all. I realized, 'Wow, my bike is showing me so much of the city.'

"On a bike it's so much different from a car because you're out in the environment and you can hear the sounds and smells. Let's face it, you don't smell a bakery or hear a shopkeeper brushing their step when you're inside a car.

"If you want to train in the most effective way, you need to not push too hard too early. Know your limits and progress one step at a time. As you build fitness, you can steadily ride harder.

"Our team is a group of people and we all work together. We all recognize our own ambitions, but we were hired to do the job that we're told to do and we all know that's the only way that we'll be successful."

Is your young rider ready for the ride? Generally speaking, in the weeks before the event, your child should at least have ridden a ride covering 80 percent of the distance of the charity ride or its longest day if it's a multiple-day ride.

COMPETITIVE ROAD RACES

Races vary from individual distance and team events to crazy-fast criterium races where riders do high-speed laps around a course of under a mile in length. The latter type in particular can be a good introduction to racing, especially if it's a practice race—meaning that a team or club is organizing the criterium as a way to prepare for an upcoming race—as it's also easy to pull out if things aren't going well. The best way to find out about road races and criteriums in your area is to talk to your local shop or cycling club—they're likely the ones organizing the events, so they'll have all the details. You can also learn about national-level events by visiting the USA Cycling Web site at www.usacycling.org.

Is your young rider ready to race? Along with being comfortable with the distance, she should also feel at ease riding in a group—she'll often be in close contact with other riders (perhaps even bumping elbows) during the event. "It's hard to just jump in and be a good racer. People can tell you what to do all day long," says Discovery Channel Team rider Tom Danielson, "but until you have some real experience under your belt, it can be tough."

NONCOMPETITIVE TRAIL RIDES

Your best bet here: a mountain bike festival. Though not as widespread as charity road rides, mountain bike festivals attract a diverse group of riders because they feature a wide variety of rides—there's something for riders of every level at a mountain bike festival. Most bike festivals are organized by local clubs and bike shops, so talk to the folks at your shop to find out details on festivals in your area, or check www.dirtrag.com.

Is your young rider ready for a festival? Aside from covering the distances of the rides he plans to do, he should know how to perform basic on-the-trail maintenance (see page 79).

COMPETITIVE TRAIL EVENTS

Options for competition abound in the off-road world—everything from high-endurance cross-country events and 24-hour races to adrenaline-pumping downhill races and awe-inspiring jump contests. While downhill races are generally held at ski resorts, cross-country and other events can take place anywhere there's a trail. Again, your local shop or bike club is the place to check for information on races in your area. Or, visit www.usacycling.org to learn about national-level events.

Is your kid ready to race? Downhill racing (and, in some cases, dirt jumping) requires specialized safety gear, such as full-face helmets and knee/shin and elbow pads. Cross-country races are high-exertion

If your teen has been working hard to prepare for an event and his desire to ride suddenly dissipates, he seems chronically tired, he complains about actually getting slower or feeling weaker on the bike, or he's irritable (more so than usual) and unwilling to work with teammates, tell him it's time to take a break. "I forget who said it, but the idea is that most people train too easy on their hard days and too hard on their easy days," says Discovery Channel Team rider Roger Hammond. "Basically, you can't go at your maximum all the time and you need to develop a finely tuned sense of what your body is telling you."

Generally speaking, teenagers—especially those who are still growing—should never train more than 20 hours a week, and they shouldn't increase the amount they train by more than 10 percent each week. Any more than that and they risk overtraining, or worse, injury. If your child shows symptoms of overtraining, have him take at least a week off to rest, and have him focus on easy rides for a few weeks once he's back on the bike.

events—though your child might be comfortable with the distance, riding at "race pace" adds another layer of difficulty to the event. Have him do some training rides at an extra-fast pace in the weeks before the event.

TOURING

Pack some camping gear, load it onto your bikes, and head out for an overnight trip (or longer) as a family. That's an oversimplification of what's required for bike touring, but there may be no better way to connect with your teen while on two wheels than by taking a few days to experience an adventure together. Treat your child as an equal on the trip, sharing the ups and downs of the trip together. And plan for plenty of downtime in camp so you can simply talk to one another, read a book, or play some games. For information on bike tours and overnight trips, check out the Adventure Cycling Association Web site, www.adv-cycling.org. For a list of bicycle touring companies, visit the League of American Bicyclists Web site at www.bikeleague.org/linkstouring.htm.

Are you and your child ready to tour? If you're cycling on an overnight trip, you'll need to carry all your gear, either on the bike or in a tow-behind trailer. Tow-behind trailers, such as the Bob Yak (www.bobtrailers.com), attach to the rear of your bike and track directly behind you. They alter the way your bike handles—namely, you won't be able to corner as sharply and the added weight means it will take longer to stop. Not up for a trailer? You can also use panniers, which are bags that attach to front and rear racks mounted onto your bike. Do some practice rides with your kid to get used to the feel of loaded panniers—as with a trailer, the extra weight will change the way your bikes handle, not to mention how quickly they stop.

GEAR: THE NEXT BIKE

The time has come. Your child's bike will no longer bear the label "kid's" or "youth." After all, your child isn't really a child anymore. As a teenager, your child is a small step away from being an adult—at least in size. As a result, her next bike will be the real thing.

IS YOUR TOWN CYCLING-FRIENDLY?

Bike routes, paths, and lanes make it easy to become an everyday cyclist, as you're simply more likely to park the car and ride if you can safely and easily bike to work, to the store, or to school. But it takes organization and perseverance to make a town bike-friendly—and it certainly doesn't happen overnight. To figure out what your first steps should be, use the BikeAbility Checklist created by the Pedestrian and Bicycle Information Center, the National Highway Traffic Safety Administration, and the U.S. Department of Transportation, which you can download at www.bicyclinginfo.org/pdf/bikabilitychecklist.pdf. Another great resource: Active Transportation (http://www.activetrans portation.org), a Web site offering lots of information on how to make human-powered transportation an everyday occurrence.

But that doesn't necessarily help when it comes to choosing and setting up the right bike. Far from it, in fact: The range of bikes available to adults is even greater than what's on the market for children. So when your son or daughter finally outgrows that 24-inch-wheeled all-around bike, you're faced with some important decisions. The biggest factor for parents, of course, is price. But remember: Though the price of a quality bike can seem steep, you should view it as an investment in your child's health. After all, cycling can keep her fit for life. And a quality bike for a teenager doesn't need to cost a fortune—as long as you're a smart shopper.

ADVICE FOR BUYING

Shopping Starts at Home Your child is ready to move on to a bigger bike; you and your spouse have adult-size bikes. You can learn a lot about your teenager's cycling inclinations if you make the connection here early ("Hey, honey, why don't we set you up on my bike for a while?"), especially if you own both a mountain bike and a road bike. Which one does your child use more often? Does she seem to have more fun on one than on the other? What does she like about the bike? Dislike about it? You can quickly narrow down your bike-shopping choices by watching your child's riding habits on your bike. Two caveats: This only works if your bike fits your teen (read on to learn how each type of bike should fit) and if your bike matches your teen's riding wishes. If your child is an aspiring dirt jumper and you only ride a touring bike, he won't even want to touch it, let alone ride it.

Be Sensible Don't have unrealistic expectations for your teen's level of interest—there's no need to rush out and buy a tricked-out high-end bike for your teenager. At least, not yet. Most high-end bikes are elegant machines that are fine-tuned for a single area of riding, and your teen likely hasn't landed in a specific cycling niche. Less-expensive bikes tend to be more general-purpose bikes that are good for letting your child develop a passion for riding. Bottom line: Don't go overboard yet. When your teen tells you that his bike is holding him back, it's time to talk about specific-interest bikes. (See "The Wide World of Bikes," page 63.)

Trust Your Bike Shop There's no better resource when you're shopping for that first full-size bike than a bike shop with a knowledgeable staff. Not only will a shop be able to help steer your teen to the type of bike that's likely to suit him best, but it'll also be able to do so within the price range you specify. Beyond that, the shop will be able to tell you about group rides in the area, give you advice on maintenance and repair, and generally offer any kind of bike-related assistance you might need. A good shop is a cyclist's best friend—make sure your teen knows it.

THE WIDE WORLD OF BIKES

Adult-size bikes come in two very large categories: road bikes and off-road bikes. There are numerous subcategories under each, and there's even some overlap in some areas (mountain bikes with slick tires that are meant for road use; or specially designed road bikes called cyclocross bikes that can handle the abuse of dirt trails). But, at this point, you shouldn't be delving into the world of niche bikes. Instead, you want your teenager to be on a bike that fits both her body and her general area of interest.

And that's where your first big decision has to occur: Will your child be better off with a road bike or a mountain bike? It's a collaborative decision—you shouldn't buy your teenager a bike without her input. Here's some advice to help make the decision easier. Happy shopping.

Road Bikes

Does your teen aspire to be the next Lance Armstrong or George Hincapie? Is there a dearth of bike-friendly trails in your area but a well-thought-out variety of bike lanes and paths? Is your child drawn to speed, but not to the technical trials of rocky, root-infested trails? If you answer yes to these questions, a road bike could be the right choice. Another big factor: Do you prefer road riding? If so, there's a good chance your teen will, as well.

Handlebar Road bikes use a distinctive, dropped-and-curved handlebar that offers the rider multiple hand positions (riding with hands in the drops, on the top of the bar, on the brake hoods, and so on). To find the right road handlebar for your teen, feel at the top of each of her shoulders for a bony "bump," then measure the distance between these two bumps—that's the ideal handlebar width.

Wheel Size The standard size for road bike wheels is "700c." Curiously, the name is simply a historical artifact: It used to be that the outside diameter of wheels would measure 700 millimeters; today, that is almost never the case, and most road wheels actually measure closer to 680 mm in outside diameter. Regardless, the wheels have a larger diameter than mountain bike wheels, and they use narrower tires. Combined with high air pressure, they allow for low rolling resistance and high speed—the perfect combination for the road.

Gearing Most road bikes use two front chainrings and nine (in some cases, 10) rear cogs, for a combination of 18 (or 20) gears. Some models offer three front chainrings; the addition of a small front chainring makes it easier to climb extra-steep hills.

Shifters and Brakes Higher-priced bikes use combination shift-and-brake levers; with everything mounted on the handlebar, the brakes and shifter are easily accessible while riding. The lever is pulled toward the bar to brake, or pushed to the side to shift (some shifters, such as those made by Campagnolo, also use a thumb-operated switch to shift in one direction, while the lever is pushed to shift in the other direction). Lower-priced bikes have shift levers mounted on the bike's downtube. This type of shifter is less mechanically complicated than integrated shift-and-brake levers, but it also requires the rider to remove a hand from the handlebar in order to shift.

Pedals Low-cost road bikes often use toe clips: plastic or steel "cages" with a fabric strap. The rider's foot slips into the cage, and the strap is tightened to hold the foot in place. Most bikes over $500 use clip-less pedals, which employ a type of click-in binding: The rider steps on the pedal, which clamps onto a cleat mounted to the bottom of cycling-specific shoes. The rider's foot is held in place until she purposefully twists out of the pedal. The super-secure binding lets the rider pull, as well as push, on the pedals, giving better power transfer. But releasing from the pedals takes some getting used to—it isn't unusual for first-timers to have a difficult time unclipping. And the pedals can cause knee injuries if the cleats aren't properly aligned—when the rider clicks in, the pedal spindle should sit directly below or just behind the ball of the foot, and the foot shouldn't be twisted too far in or out.

Frame Options Aluminum is undoubtedly the most popular frame material today, especially on bikes that are meant for first-time riders (don't disregard that label—your teen falls into this category). Aluminum is light and strong, and, when correctly used, it lasts a very long time. Carbon fiber forks are also common; more expensive bikes will also employ carbon fiber seatstays to help absorb vibration. There are a couple of other viable frame options as well. Steel is one, although high-quality steel bikes are expensive, and inexpensive steel bikes tend to be heavy. Titanium and full carbon-fiber frames are also available, though they're often prohibitively expensive, especially for a first bike.

TWO KEYS OF PROPER BIKE FIT

LEG EXTENSION This is critical to avoid knee injuries. Have your teen sit on the bike and ride around, or have someone hold him upright as he pedals backward on the bike. At the bottom of the pedal stroke, his knee should be only slightly bent; viewed from behind, his hips shouldn't rock from side to side as he pedals.

REACH Have your teen sit in the saddle and put his hands on the brake hoods with his arms straight. The angle between the top tube and his back should be around 45 degrees, and the angle between his upper body and his arms should be close to 90 degrees. This will get you in the ballpark—if all the pieces (leg extension and reach) fall into place, it's a good sign that you've found the right bike. Fit can be fine-tuned from there to whatever your teen finds comfortable.

Fit Road bikes come in a wide range of sizes, so finding a precise fit shouldn't be an issue. There's no simple "if you're this tall, you ride this size" guide, though—leg length and upper-body reach vary greatly from person to person. To get the best fit, visit a shop and try a range of bikes.

Price A brand-new starter road bike, with an aluminum frame and a carbon fork, will cost just under $600.

Mountain Bikes

Do you have lots of bike-friendly trails in your area? Do you do lots of hiking? Does your teen have an interest in jumps, drops, or technical riding? Would she feel more comfortable on a bike with a more upright position, either on road or off? If so, a mountain bike would be a smart choice.

Handlebar Most mountain bikes today come with riser bars, which are curved upward near the stem before flattening out again to accommodate the shifters, brakes, and grips. The bars allow a more upright riding position and shift the rider's weight more to the rear of the bike, which can be a benefit on downhills.

Some mountain bikes come with flat bars, which tend to be lighter and narrower than riser bars. These bars can shift more of the rider's weight to the front, which keeps the front wheel planted on climbs, giving the rider more control. The narrower bars can also be a benefit on tight trails where wider bars can get hung up.

Wheel Size Most mountain bikes use stout 26-inch wheels, though there are a few that use larger, 29-inch wheels. Tires are much wider than on a road bike—generally speaking, anywhere from just less than 2 inches to 3 (and sometimes more) inches wide. The wider tires use lower air pressure; the combination gives superb traction, though the wheels roll slower than road bike wheels.

Gearing Most mountain bikes have three chainrings in the front and nine cogs in the rear, for a total of 27 gears. The bikes use lower gearing than road bikes, which makes it easier to climb extra-steep pitches on the trail.

Shifters and Brakes Mountain bikes utilize a variety of shifters: twist-type shifters, where part of the grip rotates to initiate a shift; and trigger shifters, where levers are pressed by the thumb (and sometimes the index finger) to shift; or integrated shift/brake levers, where the brake lever is moved up or down by the fingers to shift. First-timer bikes generally use twist-type or trigger shifters.

Brakes can be either rim brakes, where the brake pads squeeze the sides of the wheel's rims to slow the bike, or disc brakes, where a brake caliper clamps to a rotor attached to the wheel's hub to slow the bike. Rim brakes are generally less expensive than disc brakes, though disc brakes tend to be more powerful stoppers.

Suspension Almost all mountain bikes utilize front suspension, which allows the front wheel to move up and down over obstacles on the trail and gives the rider greater control with less fatigue. More expensive mountain bikes also often use rear suspension, which allows the rear wheel to move up and down over trail obstacles. Whichever type of suspension your teen chooses, make sure it is adjusted to match her weight—which requires either releasing or adding air to an air shock or fork, or changing the spring in a coil sprung shock or fork. Beyond that, the fork or shock should at least have adjustable rebound damping, so she can control the rate at which the suspension returns to the normal riding position after hitting a bump.

Pedals As with road bikes, mountain bike pedals can use toe clips or be the clipless variety, but there's another option that sees use in some areas of mountain biking: flat pedals (those with no retention mechanism). Many dirt jumpers, freeriders, and downhillers use flat pedals, which have no way to hold the rider's foot to the pedal. Small metal pins on the pedal offer traction and help keep the rider's feet in place. The main benefit of flat pedals is that, if things get out of control, the rider can easily get off and away from the bike.

Frame Options Mountain bike frames usually come in one of two varieties: hardtail (which generally use front suspension but have a solid rear triangle) and full-suspension (which uses both front and rear suspension). Almost all mid-priced mountain bikes, whether hardtail or full-suspension, have frames made of aluminum. As with road bikes, other frame materials, such as steel, carbon fiber, and titanium, can also be used, although aluminum frames tend to offer the best overall value of price and performance.

Fit As with road bikes, the two most important aspects of mountain bike fit are leg extension and reach. However, there are a few distinct points to keep in mind.

The same key points of leg extension still apply: The rider should have a slight bend in her knee at the bottom of the pedal stroke, and her hips shouldn't rock from side to side as she pedals. On a mountain bike, though, it can be a benefit to be able to drop the saddle out of the way for tricky descents. So, make sure that the saddle can be extended to allow for proper pedaling, but that it can be dropped at least 6 inches to get out of the way for tough descents.

A road-bike-type reach is perfect for faster, cross-country riding and racing. A more upright position (slightly greater than 45 degrees between your teen's back and the top tube of the bike) gives greater control in technical situations, such as riding over rocks, roots, and other obstacles. The right reach depends on the type of trails your teen will be riding on most.

Price Basic performance-oriented, aluminum-framed hardtails with disc brakes are available for around $500; rim-brake versions cost even less. A similarly equipped entry-level full-suspension bike costs nearly twice as much.

HOW TO SHOP SMART

The number-one place to buy a first bike for a teenager? A bike shop. The expertise of bike shop employees is priceless, and you'll often get free maintenance (a great deal, since shifters and brakes often need tweaking after a few initial break-in rides) and service for up to a year if you buy through a shop.

If you want to save some cash on the purchase price, don't resort to a big-box store for a high-performance bike. Instead, look for a used bike. eBay (www.ebay.com) and Craig's List (www.craigslist.com)

are good web-based options, while many urban areas have "bike swaps," which are basically flea markets for cyclists. Your teen will be able to try the bike before you buy to make sure it fits—a must, and one of the reasons why online shopping isn't a smart move, at least while you're deciphering the perfect fit of a first bike. Want to find a bike swap in your area? Ask the employees at your local shop. Who knows—they might even have a used bike for sale.

FRINGE BIKES

CYCLOCROSS Specially designed, super-versatile road bikes that, among other minor adjustments, use knobby tires and super-strong brakes so that they can be used—and raced—off-road.

DOWNHILL Single-purpose mountain bikes utilizing front and rear suspension with loads (up to 10 inches) of travel. Designed to ride down steep, very technical terrain at high speeds, downhill bikes are too heavy and lack the gearing to be pedaled uphill. Freeride bikes often use similar amounts of travel, but they have the gearing to be pedaled (albeit slowly) uphill as well as down.

FIXED GEAR Also called a "track bike," a fixed gear is a road bike that utilizes only a front chainring and a single rear cog. There's no coasting on a track bike—when the wheels turn, the cranks turn, and vice versa. The rider uses her legs—not brakes—to slow (and stop) the bike.

SINGLESPEED Similar to a fixed gear, but has a freewheel so the rider can coast. Though road bikes can be singlespeeds, the term generally refers to mountain bikes.

JUMP BIKES Mountain bikes with a BMX heritage; these 26-inch-wheeled bikes have minimal front suspension and are built burly and strong to handle the forces of big jumps and harsh landings.

THE FULL KIT

Style and function go hand in hand when it comes to cycling clothes. Not surprisingly, different fashions work best with different bikes and riding styles.

One for the Road Road cyclists typically wear tight-fitting Lycra shorts and a form-fitting jersey. The clothing doesn't bunch up anywhere, and it doesn't get caught in the wind so there's no fabric flapping in the wind and slowing you down.

On the Mountain Speedy cross-country racers often opt for tight-fitting gear, for similar reasons—the form-fitting, lightweight gear won't bunch up anywhere or get caught on anything on the trail. However, riders not concerned with speed often opt for baggy shorts, which look better and can offer greater protection in a crash, matched with loose-fitting jerseys.

SKILLS: BEYOND THE BASICS

It is far too easy to overcomplicate cycling. Think about it—most 5-year-olds can develop a solid grasp on the basics: Pedal to move forward. Stop pedaling and you coast, and eventually slow down. Apply the brakes to stop. Lean and turn the handlebar slightly to go around corners. It's blissfully simple.

But while the basics are easily mastered, there are thousands of minor details—changes in body position, weight distribution, gear selection, and more—that can help a rider cover greater distances with less effort and more speed, and make the ride safer to boot. For many riders, the finer points of bike handling are learned over time, through experience. But you can help speed up your teen's bike-handling prowess by working on the following skills.

CLIMBING ON THE ROAD

Seated climbing uses less energy than standing, so have your young rider pedal in a seated position for as long as he can. It's generally thought that a pedaling cadence of 90 revolutions per minute (RPM) or higher is most efficient—a lower cadence taxes the leg muscles more; a significantly higher cadence stresses the aerobic system. (How can you tell if you're in that range? You need to get the feel for it. Take a stopwatch on a ride, start it, then count 30 crank revolutions. At the end of 30 revolutions, check the watch. If 20 seconds have passed, you're pedaling at 90 RPM.) Shift gears as often as necessary to stay in that range while you climb. Focus on pulling up on the pedals as much as pushing down.

While not as efficient as climbing while seated, standing on an ascent can give your young rider more power—great for surges of speed or for motoring over the last part of a climb when he's having a hard time turning the pedals while seated. It's okay for him to rock the bike from side to side as he climbs, but he should try to keep his body centered.

CLIMBING OFF-ROAD

Many of the same principles apply, though there's an added challenge: traction. When your child is climbing on loose dirt or other areas where she might slip, she can keep the rear wheel from spinning out by shifting into a harder gear—even though that means a lower cadence and greater muscle stress. She should stay in the saddle as much as possible, and lean her upper body forward to keep the front wheel on the ground. When she stands, remind her to purposefully think about her weight distribution—focus her weight over the rear wheel, and bend her upper body over the front of the bike to keep the front end down. To increase traction even more, she can pull back and down on the handlebar as she climbs.

CORNERING ON THE ROAD

As your child approaches a corner, he should lower the outside pedal (the left pedal in a right-hand turn) and gently apply both brakes to slow to the speed he can safely maintain through the corner. Though he can use the brakes as he corners, it's best for him to do the majority of the braking before the turn so that he doesn't lose traction when he leans the bike over. As he corners, have him focus his weight on the outside pedal; he should push himself up off the saddle slightly.

Have him look where he wants to go, and lean the bike into the turn. Some riders find it helpful to stick out the inside knee (right turn, right knee); your kid can experiment to see what works best for him. Remind him to look well ahead as he approaches a corner, so he can spot loose gravel or other roadside debris that could cause him to lose traction and crash. If he spots debris, he should slow well down beforehand and, if possible, avoid leaning the bike over in the turn.

CORNERING ON THE TRAIL

Cornering on a mountain bike is usually much slower than on a road bike, but the principles are the same: weight the outside pedal, do the majority of your braking before the turn, lean the bike into the turn, and look where you want to go. One additional tip to share with your child: As he leans his bike into the turn, he should keep his body-weight centered on the bike, directly over where the tires contact the ground. This can increase traction in a turn and help him keep control when traction is iffy.

BRAKING—ROAD AND MOUNTAIN

It's easy to be intimidated by the front brake. After all, grabbing a handful of rear brake only causes the rear wheel to skid, while slamming on the front brake can send you flying over the handlebar. But it's that same outstanding power that makes the front brake so effective; it's estimated that about 75 percent of total braking power comes from the front brake.

When a rider hits the brakes—either brake—her weight shifts to the front of the bike. This unweights the rear wheel, and the resulting loss of traction allows it to skid. And that means she's not slowing down very effectively. However, that same weight shift gives the front wheel *more* traction, which is what makes it such a powerful stopper. The general rule with brakes: Use the rear brake to reduce speed, but use the front brake to stop in a hurry. When your child is braking, tell her to stand on the pedals and shift her weight to the rear of the bike, or even behind the saddle in extreme situations. Be cautious when braking in loose conditions or on wet pavement—skidding the front wheel almost always results in a crash.

Back off. Chances are you've been pushing cycling onto your child a little too forcefully. Give your teen space, but continue to ride and be a role model for the cycling lifestyle. Even if your teen rebels against cycling now, he'll always remember your passion for the sport—and he'll still be influenced by the healthy lifestyle decisions you make. Remember, he may pick up the sport again later on.

OBSTACLES ON THE ROAD

Obstacles encountered on the road tend to be small—and deceptively tricky. Three of the most common are sticks, gravel, and potholes.

With sticks, size and orientation are the biggest factors to consider. The best way to handle smaller sticks (up to an inch or so) is to get your weight to the back of the bike and ride over them. But swerve to avoid sticks that are lying parallel to your direction of travel: they can snag a wheel and make you crash. For larger sticks, your best bet is to bunnyhop them (see page 74).

Gravel isn't an issue if you're traveling straight. If you try to turn in a patch of gravel, however, you're going to slide. And that can make you lose control. If your teen can travel straight through a patch of gravel, tell him to do so—have him brake before he enters the patch, and shift his weight to the rear of the bike as he goes through. If he needs to turn, he should slow way down beforehand, stay loose, and make his way through the turn.

Usually, riders become aware of potholes in plenty of time to avoid them, and that's the best thing to do if it's possible. (But don't veer into traffic to avoid a pothole.) If a pothole sneaks up on a rider, though, his best bet is to bunnyhop it (see "The Bunnyhop," page 74). At the very least, he should yank the front wheel up and over the hole—he may slam the rear wheel into the hole and get a flat tire, but he'll likely walk away unscathed.

OBSTACLES ON THE TRAIL

Obstacles are what make mountain biking exciting. Rocks, roots, logs, you name it: Most everything on the trail is fair game to a mountain bike. The key to attempting—and eventually clearing—most any obstacle is the basic "attack" position.

Here's how you, or your teen, can do it.

Stand with the pedals level. Flex your knees and elbows, but keep some tension—you want them to absorb impact as well as hold you up. Bend your upper body forward slightly to keep your weight centered on the bike. You should feel like you're about to pounce, because you are. From this position, you can easily shift your weight back for technical downhills, apply power to the pedals for climbs or to negotiate smaller rocks, or pull up on the front of the bike to lift it onto obstacles. From this stance, anything is possible.

THE BUNNYHOP

There are two types of bunnyhop. With one, the rider depends on his clipless pedals to pull the bike into the air; with the other, the rider depends on technique to loop the bike into the air. Here's how they work.

Bunnyhopping with clipless pedals is easy. First, have your child stand on the pedals in the attack position while traveling slightly faster than walking speed (she can increase speed as her skills improve). She should crouch down to force her weight into the bike, then quickly spring up, using her hands and arms to pull up and back on the handlebar as her legs pull the bike up. At first, she'll likely only pull the bike a few inches into the air, but with practice, she'll be able to raise it higher. Tell your teen: Don't simply hop straight up—think "forward" to get yourself up and over an obstacle.

Bunnyhopping without clipless pedals happens in more of an arc. Have your child stand on the pedals with the pedals level, traveling at slightly faster than walking speed. She should lean back and lift the front end of the bike into the air. Then, she should quickly shift her weight forward as she pushes forward with her arms and scoops the rear of the bike into the air with her feet. She can practice on small objects to get a feel for the technique.

FALLING

All cyclists eventually crash. That's why we wear helmets. But even minor falls (such as toppling over at a stop sign because you didn't clip out of your pedals in time) can result in injury—if you don't know the right way to fall.

Too often, our instincts work against us when we fall. We naturally want to catch ourselves as we're going over, so we put our hands out—and that can lead to some of cycling's most common injuries: broken wrists, arms, and collarbones.

There are two ways that your child can protect himself during a crash. One is to get away from the bike—step off to the side and push it away, slide off the back and push it away, etc. Number two is to be a ball—he should pull his arms in to his body and roll to dissipate the energy of the fall. Rolling out of a crash can save both flesh and bones in even the hardest fall. It's one skill that no rider should be without. Don't be afraid to have your young riders practice falling on soft grass—as with everything, practice does make perfect.

NIGHT RIDING

Trails in the dark can be great fun—as long as they're properly lit, that is. Bright, rechargeable bike lights are available that can be attached to the handlebar or to your child's helmet. At up to $500, the lights aren't cheap, but, if your kid wants to ride at night, they're a necessity.

The tunnel of visibility created by a bike light leads to one of the most interesting sensations of night riding. The lack of peripheral vision forces the rider to focus on what's in front of him, which increases reaction time and, in turn, improves bike-handling skills.

Night requires a few minor adaptations. First, riders need to stay closer to the center of the trail, especially in corners, since it can be hard to judge obstacles on the edges of the light's beam. Second, be aware that a ride should last only as long as your battery power, and leave some juice to spare. Most lights will run for at least an hour, if not longer. Once you know how long your lights will last, plan to leave a quarter of that time as a reserve—if the battery will last for 60 minutes, the ride shouldn't last longer than 45 minutes. And always carry a backup light, such as a small LED headlamp, just in case. Remember, night rides are as fraught with danger as any other type of riding so be equipped with the proper safety gear, including a mobile phone and accompany your child after dark.

WINTER RIDING

While riding in cold weather simply means additional layers of clothing to stay warm, ice and snow require different riding techniques. "I always wear a number of layers and carry extra, including a pair of thick mitts, in my pocket," says Michael Barry of the Discovery Channel Team, a Boulder, Colorado–based rider who spends his share of time in the cold. "I also have a rule: If the snow is covering the road, I turn around and head home."

Ice is scary. Period. To cross a patch of ice safely, keep your weight centered, don't touch your brakes, and apply even pressure to the pedals—don't try to accelerate, or your rear wheel will slip. Stay centered and loose on the bike to absorb any minor slides, and work your way directly to the other side. If ice is a constant problem where you and your teenager ride, studded tires can provide a real benefit—the metal rivets in the tires will grab onto ice and give you traction.

Snow, in the right conditions, is fun. You can easily crunch through a couple of inches of powder on top of the ground without changing your riding style much, though it will take more energy to pedal and also take longer to brake. If the snow gets much deeper, however, it becomes almost impossible to ride in—unless it gets packed down. On a packed snow trail, lower the air pressure in the bike's tires slightly to increase traction (there's little risk of pinch flatting on a snow-covered trail), travel at a slightly slower-than-normal speed, and keep your weight to the rear of the bike. Too much weight on the front can cause the front wheel to punch through the snow and stop abruptly. Remember, too, that brakes, even discs, probably won't feel as strong in the snow, as ice could build up on the braking surfaces. But don't worry too much about that—just enjoy the snowy trails.

MAINTENANCE: THE ESSENTIALS AND MORE

A well-maintained bike is a work of art. But it isn't art that's meant to hang on a wall; it's performance art. The gleaming parts offer crisp, precise shifting and smooth, easily controlled braking. The cranks rotate fluidly, with little friction. The wheels sing along the pavement or flow along the trail. The suspension effortlessly soaks up bumps and chatter.

As a cyclist, you know that it takes work to keep your bike working its best. You also know that, while some parts of bike maintenance and repair are best left to professional mechanics, there are many important, essential bits of maintenance that you can do yourself. It's time for your teen to learn that same lesson. Explain that home maintenance can save money, as you aren't paying a mechanic for every little thing that goes wrong. And make sure that your teen knows the essentials of on-the-road repair. After all, that can make the difference between *riding* home and *walking* home.

TOOL-FREE TUNE-UP SKILLS

Brakes Give the brakes a squeeze as part of every preride check. If you can move the lever all the way to the bar, it's time to make a quick adjustment.

On mountain bikes with linear-pull brakes, there's a barrel-shaped adjuster where the brake cable exits the lever. Turn this barrel counterclockwise for two or three turns, then squeeze the levers again. Still hitting the bar? Turn the adjuster some more. Still hitting the bar? Check the brake pads. If they're worn out—the pad is worn nearly flat against the aluminum brake-pad holder—you and your teen need to replace the pads before she can safely ride again. Head to your local bike shop together to buy some pads.

Does your child's mountain bike have disc brakes? If the brakes are mechanical (meaning there's a cable running from the lever to the caliper), adjust the brake pad position closer to the rotor—on most mechanical disc brakes, there's a pad adjuster on the caliper bodies attached to the frame (in the rear) and the fork (in the front). You may also need to give a counterclockwise turn to the barrel adjuster on the brake lever. If the brakes are hydraulic (meaning there's a sealed brake line full of fluid, and not a brake cable, actuating the brakes), check to see whether the pads are worn. The pads are located in the caliper bodies attached to the frame (in the rear) and fork (in the front). If the braking surface on the pads is thinner than a dime, the pads should be replaced. If the pads are fine, there could be air in the brake line. You'll need to bleed the brakes before your child can safely ride again. Head to the bike shop for brake fluid, or to have the brakes bled.

On road bikes, the brake's barrel adjuster is on the brake itself. Use the same counterclockwise turns to adjust the brakes, and check the pads if you need to. *Note:* On some brakes, there's a quick-release lever that moves the brake arms apart so the wheel can be removed. Make sure that lever is closed before you adjust the brakes.

Derailleurs Have your teen take a short spin and shift through his bike's gears. Is the chain slow to shift? Does it refuse to go into the top- or bottommost gears in the rear, or does it grind noisily in the front? Give the derailleurs a quick tweak. Here's how.

If his front derailleur won't move the chain onto the big chainring, first check that he isn't cross-chaining—meaning he isn't trying to shift into a big chainring/big cog combination. In some cases, the extreme angle of this type of shift can keep the chain from engaging. If that isn't the issue, give the barrel adjuster (on mountain bikes, it's on the shifter; on road bikes, it's located on the frame's downtube) a counterclockwise spin; today's derailleurs and shifters are sensitive enough that you won't need to spin the adjuster much to make a difference—one half-turn should do it. Then, check that the chain still shifts into the smallest chainring; if it doesn't, spin the barrel adjuster clockwise a quarter-turn. If you can't make the adjustment work, it could be time to head to the shop. With between 18 and 30 speeds on a typical bike, derailleur adjustments can be difficult to master.

If the rear derailleur isn't shifting into the right gear, first check that it is bolted securely to the frame—use a 5-millimeter Allen wrench to tighten it down, and check the shifting again. If the derailleur won't move into the uppermost cogs, turn the barrel adjuster (on mountain bikes, it's located either where the shift cable exits the rear derailleur, or where the cable exits the shifter; on road bikes, it's located either where the cable exits the rear derailleur, or on the frame's downtube) counterclockwise a half-turn, and check the shifting. Repeat as necessary. If the derailleur won't move to the lowermost cogs, give the barrel adjuster a clockwise turn. If you can't make the adjustments work or if you've simply made things worse, it could be time to head to the shop.

OUT THERE REPAIR

Fix a Flat The most common bit of maintenance is fixing a flat. With the right knowledge and a little practice, you and your teen will be able to swap tubes in a matter of 5 minutes or less. Here's how.

Remove the wheel from the bike (if it's the rear tire, first shift to the smallest cog to make it easier to get the wheel back on). Squeeze the sides of the tire toward the center of the rim to help unseat the tire from the rim. Insert a tire lever under the edge of the tire opposite the valve stem, and hook the other end of the lever around a spoke. Insert a second lever a few inches away, and pop the tire bead over the rim. You should be able to slide the second lever along between the rim and tire to further unseat the tire; if not, insert a third tire lever. At that point, you should be able to unseat the rest of that side of the tire by hand.

With one side of the tire completely free of the rim, reach in and grab the tube near the valve stem. Pull the stem back out of the valve hole in the rim; once it's free, you can remove the tube completely. Pump up the tube slightly to see if you can pinpoint the source of the leak—you'll want to remove any debris in the tire casing that might have caused the puncture.

Once that's done, put the old tube in your pocket (you can patch it later) and get out your spare. Remove the valve cap and nut, and give the tube a few shots from your pump so that it has some shape. Install the tube on the wheel, starting with the valve. Slide the valve through the rim's valve hole, and slowly work your way around the wheel, sliding the tube into place both inside the tire and on the rim. Once it's in place, you can reinstall the tire.

Start with the wheel in your lap, with the valve closest to you. Use both hands, and hook the tire bead into place at the valve. Then,

Basic bicycle repair is easy to master, even for a young rider.

slowly work your hands up the sides of the tire, pushing the tire bead onto the center of the rim. At the top, grab the tire tightly with both hands, and roll the last bit of it into place—it takes a lot of effort, but the tire should "pop" into place on the rim. Use tire levers as a last resort; they can easily puncture the tube. Once the tire is on, pump up the tube, reinstall it on your bike, and you're off.

Repair a Chain With a chain tool, your kid can repair most any broken chain well enough to get home. Here's how to do it. First, inspect the chain to evaluate the damage; chances are, one of the outer plates on one link of the chain is bent. Use the chain tool to push out the rivet holding the damaged link in place: Unwind the tool so that the rivet you hope to push out will sit in the tool body, in the slot farthest away from the tool handle. Tighten the handle, and check that the tool's pin is aligned directly with the rivet you want to push out (if it isn't, you could break the tool's pin instead of your chain). Then, tighten the handle (it could take some effort) to push the rivet out.

Here's the key, though: Unless you have a spare SRAM Power Connector (an easy-to-use, hand-removable "master" link) to replace the broken link, you need to make sure that the ends of the chain will fit together: One end should be the inner plates and roller, and the other should be the outer plates—and the chain rivet should be attached to one of those outer plates.

If you're removing a broken link, it's likely that you'll want to reuse the rivet you're pushing out. So don't push it out completely. As you turn the handle on the chain tool, keep checking the progress of the rivet—you only want to push it far enough so that you can remove the damaged link. Once that bent link is removed, you can reattach the two ends of the chain.

First, make sure you thread the chain through the derailleurs correctly—you don't want to have to break the chain apart and reattach it again. Once that's done, slide the two ends of the chain together, and push the inner plates into place. With any luck, the tail end of the rivet (the one you're about to push back through the link) will stick out enough to hold the inner links in place. Then, align the pin in your chain tool with the end of the rivet, and turn the handle to push the rivet back into place. You'll feel more and more resistance as you push; keep turning until the pin sticks out an equal distance from both sides of the chain. Then loosen the tool.

Most likely, the newly rejoined link won't rotate as freely as the rest of the chain. Grab the chain tightly on each side of the tight link, and bend it back and forth horizontally a few times to loosen the link.

THE HOME MECHANIC

Several companies sell high-quality bike tools, including complete tool sets for the home mechanic. The sets vary in size from very basic (hex keys, patch kits, screwdrivers, and adjustable wrenches) to everything a professional mechanic might need.

Don't want to buy a full tool set? That's fine—they're expensive, after all—but there are still several must-have tools that make every repair job easier. So if you're building a family tool kit from scratch, start with these, and add other tools as you need them.

- Adjustable wrench

- Cable and housing cutter. Cuts cleaner than a typical wire cutter, which is essential for smooth shifting and braking.

WHAT TO CARRY

There are a few essential tools that your teen should carry on every ride. With these, she can fix almost anything that goes wrong with her bike in the field, if not permanently, then at least well enough that she can ride home.

CASH Because you never know.

CELL PHONE Tell your teen not to use it lightly—and not while riding. In an emergency, though, a cell phone can be a lifesaver.

FOLDING HEX KEY SET Most available bike-specific folding Allen wrench sets contain other necessary tools, including a chain tool, spoke wrenches, and Phillips- and flat-head screwdrivers.

- Hex wrench set. Those with a T- or P-handle are a smart buy, as they offer a good mix of fit and leverage.

- Pedal wrench

- Phillips- and flat-head screwdrivers

- Workstand. Holds the bike steady at an easy-to-reach height.

· ·

MINI-PUMP To pump up a tire. Most fit easily in a hydration pack; they can also be stowed in a jersey pocket.

· ·

PATCH KIT If your teen gets more than one flat, she needs to be able to repair her tube. *Note:* Glueless patches are fast and easy to use, but they don't always adhere as well as glue-on patches.

· ·

TIRE LEVERS Carry a minimum of two high-quality plastic levers; cheap levers can break. In a pinch, using the quick-release levers from the wheels can do the job.

· ·

TUBE Replacing a tube in the field is often faster than patching a hole in a tube.

· ·

....

PART V

NUTRITION

Building Healthy Habits for the Future

....

WHY IS IT IMPORTANT FOR YOUR CHILD TO EAT A PROPER DIET?

Proper nutrition is one factor that can contribute to making sports a positive experience for kids. If young athletes are well-hydrated and adequately fueled, they will get more out of their rides and everything else they do for the remainder of the day. Once you understand the nutritional needs of your children, you can focus on teaching them to learn how to be healthy, make good choices, and form habits that will serve them in the future—regardless of whether they become serious athletes.

Just like adults, young athletes need adequate nutrition to maintain health and optimize performance. To complete their rides effectively, children need fuel to keep their bodies moving. Food replenishes the energy burned while pedaling. By eating high-quality meals and topping off energy supplies as they are consumed, your child will be able to ride stronger and longer, stay mentally alert, and finish his ride happy and ready to go back out for the next epic. He'll also recover more quickly from training or competition.

The young rider who is not taking in enough energy or who isn't eating correctly is put at risk of wilting and not enjoying the sport. "Bonking"—running so low on available energy that the body simply shuts down all excessive activity—is every bit as unpleasant for children as it is for adults. When inadequate nutrition—eating too little, or not enough of the right things—is a chronic problem, young riders may also suffer from poor bone growth and delayed maturation.

Children who exercise regularly put additional demands on their bodies. They require more nutrient-rich calories to replace those burned during exercise, for recovery following exercise, and to build strong muscles, bones, and joints. Part of the postride recovery process is replenishment of glycogen, the body's main energy source for exercise. Glycogen is stored in the liver and muscles, aiding in muscle repair and growth and enhancing the immune system to protect the body from exercise stresses as well as from invading bacteria, viruses, and other pathogens.

In addition to assisting his sporting performances, a child's nutritional intake is responsible for his overall health, growth, and development. Adolescence, in particular, places a lot of demands on the body due to dramatic changes in body composition and stature. Your child must have adequate nutrition for these growth spurts to occur normally.

WHY IS IT IMPORTANT FOR YOUR CHILD TO BE PROPERLY HYDRATED?

Proper hydration—absorbing and maintaining adequate fluids—is arguably even more important than proper nutrition for young riders because their bodies do not regulate body temperature as efficiently as adults' bodies do. When a young athlete becomes dehydrated—lacking sufficient fluid content in the cells and bloodstream to control body temperature and cool working muscles—her aerobic performance will be compromised, but that's the least of her problems. Too little fluid in her body results in an elevated heart rate and difficulty controlling core temperature. Children overheat faster than adults do, and when dehydrated, they'll feel as if they are working harder than they really are.

You can avoid dehydration by drinking before you're thirsty.

To further complicate matters, kids almost never drink enough on their own to prevent dehydration; they tend to drink only when they are thirsty. They're just like grown-ups in this respect—impatient, distracted, and just plain too busy to drop what they're doing for a few sips of water.

To avoid dehydration, have your child drink frequently. Without overdoing it, see if you can get her to drink even more than seems necessary. Remember that, as with everything else in a young rider's life, you're the role model; show her the best possible habits by drinking continually yourself.

To encourage your child to take in adequate amounts of fluid, offer beverages that are more palatable. Cool, flavored drinks that contain simple carbohydrates (various forms of sugar, in small amounts) and a little salt work well, because they stimulate thirst and increase fluid consumption. These supplemented fluids will help to minimize the electrolytes lost through sweating. (Electrolytes are minerals—sodium, potassium, calcium, and others—that are essential to the basic operations of cells and organs throughout the body.) Contraction and relaxation of muscle tissue, for example, is impossible without the correct balance of these ions. The extra liquid-based carbohydrates in these sorts of drinks will also help fuel your child's activity.

Many sports drinks work well, and they usually contain half the sugar and calories of juice or soft drinks, and none of the carbonation. The key with sports drinks is to mix them right. They're designed to have concentrations that improve gastric emptying and uptake of nutrients, so diluting them or mixing them stronger

SOFT DRINKS SLOW YOUR YOUNG RIDER

Carbonated soft drinks are best left completely out of your child's diet. The carbonation causes a "burning" sensation in your child's mouth—the feeling that keeps him from gulping it down. Soft drinks can also cause bloating. But those are the least offensive of their many negative effects. Worse are the complications that accompany the ingestion of phosphoric acid, high fructose corn syrup, and caffeine, common soft drink ingredients.

Soft drinks are high in phosphorus and phosphoric acid, which cause calcium to be extracted from bones. This may eventually lead to osteoporosis, which is among the most serious health problems now affecting aging adults in America.

Another drawback of soft drinks is the common inclusion of high fructose corn syrup (HFCS), which has been implicated in a variety of diseases and illnesses. One such ailment thought to be the result of HFCS consumption is childhood obesity—the number one health calamity in American life. HFCS is a synthetic, high-octane sugar that seems to evade normal satiety mechanisms in the brain so that your child, quite literally, doesn't know when to stop.

actually prevents them from working optimally. Juice is a fine choice immediately following a workout; if consumed during the ride, its high sugar content can slow fluid absorption and increase the chance of a bad tummyache.

Although children sweat just like adults, they have a lower rate of sweat production and a higher rate of body heat production during physical activity. For these reasons, it is especially important to carefully monitor your child's hydration level when the weather is hot. Make sure he's extra-hydrated by doubling his usual liquid intake before he hops on a bike, while he's on the road or trail (with plain water and beverages that contain sugar and electrolytes), and after the ride is over. Be very diligent about his drinking on regular intervals throughout the ride. This will have the added benefit of keeping you tuned in to your own hydration.

· ·

HFCS is made from corn syrup by converting glucose into fructose using an enzymatic process. When you ingest simple carbohydrates such as glucose, your pancreas releases more insulin to help control further sugar consumption by sending a sense of fullness to your brain. Unfortunately, the fructose in HFCS gets around the triggering mechanism, which can lead a person to eat more sugar and calories before getting the signal to stop.

What's more, HFCS converts more readily to fat than glucose does, because it contains a different chain of carbons. (Glucose is the form of sugar used directly by the muscles and brain.) And that may contribute to heart disease: When HFCS is converted into fat, it is stored within the cells, organs, or in adipose (fat) tissue. But in order to get to its new home, these fat molecules must be moved through the bloodstream. When extra fat is meandering through the blood, it can aid in the buildup of plaque, which clogs arteries.

Lastly, soft drinks often contain caffeine, which can also cause headaches, nausea, and agitation in kids.

· ·

When it is very hot and humid, consider cutting rides short. Heatstroke, though unusual, is possible; and the effects of sunburn are far worse when fluid intake is insufficient. Even cramping, a relatively minor concern in the grand scheme of things, will at least make the riding experience unpleasant.

Overexertion or prolonged exercise—more than 30 minutes on the bike—can also challenge your child's ability to remain hydrated. If you're cycling with your children, exemplify the good habit you're trying to instill: Stop and slake your thirst, and urge them to do the same.

EATING FOR OPTIMAL GROWTH AND PERFORMANCE

A young athlete's diet is similar to that of an adult; both need to eat a variety of foods that provide 60 to 70 percent carbohydrates, 20 to 30 percent fat, and 10 to 15 percent protein. Each of these categories plays a role in fueling the young athlete and maintaining healthy, functional organs.

CARBOHYDRATES

Carbohydrates (natural compounds composed of starches and sugars) are the main fuel used for cycling—they're the muscle's preferred energy source. Carbohydrates should compose the bulk of extra energy required by active kids. Your body makes use of carbohydrates by converting them into glycogen (the most easily assimilated energy source) and storing it in your liver and skeletal muscles. Most kids have enough stored glycogen to provide energy for short athletic activities, but for longer rides they need to eat carbohydrates to keep their energy levels high by replenishing glycogen stores. Eating too few carbohydrates can result in depleted glycogen stores, leading to fatigue.

Complex carbohydrates are the best form of carbohydrates to include in your child's diet because they supply the body with sustained energy. Complex carbohydrates get their name from their complex, chainlike structure made mostly of long strands of simple sugars. A single complex carbohydrate molecule may contain anywhere from 300 to 1,000 simple sugar units. When digested, these

The optimal diet for a young cyclist contains 60 to 70 percent carbohydrates, 20 to 30 percent fat, and 10 to 15 percent protein.

WHICH MEAL IS THE MOST IMPORTANT?

Eating a solid breakfast is the easiest, best way to keep glycogen stores high. Each night, while your child is sleeping, about 40 percent of his glycogen is burned, leaving his "tank" only 60 percent full. To keep the body moving all day, your child's breakfast should consist mainly of carbohydrates to replace the lost glycogen. Although some kids don't like to eat breakfast—perhaps because many parents aren't the best role models in this respect—they will appreciate it later in the day, in their after-school bike rides, or during their races on the weekend.

strands are broken down for use as energy. Some of the resulting simple sugars are used for instant energy, while some are used to top off glycogen stores for later use. Simple sugars also typically contain many essential nutrients.

Some quality sources of complex carbohydrates are:

- Starchy vegetables such as peas, corn, lima beans, winter squashes, and root vegetables such as potatoes and yams. Vegetables are also a good source of vitamins and minerals such as vitamin C, beta-carotene, and other antioxidants that will protect your child's body from exercise stresses. Other nutritional benefits include calcium, iron, fiber, and a bit of protein.

- Legumes such as beans, peas, and lentils. They're also a good source of protein, fiber, iron, calcium, and B vitamins.

- Whole grains such as whole wheat, rye, oats, rice, and whole grain breads, cereals, and pastas. They are rich in zinc, fiber, and B vitamins, and they also contain a bit of protein.

FATS

Although they're the most concentrated source of energy in foods, fats, thanks to their complexity, are the secondary fuel used by an athlete's body. As your child's fitness increases, his ability to break down and burn fat for energy will also improve. He'll still burn both carbohydrate and fat at all times, but fat will play an important role in conserving his limited carbohydrate stores for when they are truly needed. This comes in handy when your child is out for an endurance ride; because his body doesn't have to depend solely on quickly depleted carbohydrate stores, he can exercise longer before exhaustion sets in.

Aside from providing calories for energy and flavor, fat supplies essential fatty acids needed for recovery and to build muscle. It also provides the raw materials that help in the control of blood pressure, blood clotting, inflammation, and other body functions. Another important role of fat is to aid in the absorption and transport, through the bloodstream, of fat-soluble vitamins A, D, E, and K.

Although all fats are made up of carbon, hydrogen, and oxygen, they are not all equal. Be choosy about the types of fat your child consumes.

Saturated Fat What makes saturated fat an unhealthful diet choice is its atomic structure—there are only single bonds between the carbon atoms due to its saturation of hydrogen molecules. Without the presence of double bonds, saturated fats are difficult to break down into a usable resource for the body.

Saturated fats have also been shown to raise the level of low-density lipoprotein (LDL, or "bad cholesterol") in the blood, which increases the risk of heart disease. As if that weren't bad enough, they also decrease levels of high-density lipoprotein (HDL, or "good cholesterol"). HDL helps with the removal of cholesterol (a major contributor to arterial plaque) from the arteries.

Saturated fat is a solid at room temperature and occurs naturally mostly in animal products such as butter and other dairy items, red meat, and poultry (especially dark meat).

Saturated fat can also be created by converting unsaturated fat to its saturated form through a process called hydrogenation, in which hydrogen molecules are forced into the carbon bonds, breaking the double (unsaturated) bonds and leaving the molecule with all single (saturated) bonds.

These resulting hydrogenated oils can be found in processed foods such as candy bars, potato chips, and other prepackaged food items.

Trans Fatty Acids These fats start off as unsaturated oils but undergo only a partial hydrogenation—just enough to stabilize the oils to prevent them from becoming rancid (so the product in which they'll eventually be used will have a longer shelf life) and to keep them solid at room temperature.

Trans fatty acids are dangerous for the heart and may pose a risk for certain cancers because they behave like saturated fat. Partially hydrogenated oils contain trans fat, but the fully hydrogenated oils mentioned above are actually trans fat free; they're just made into artery-clogging saturated fat. Additionally, omega-3 fatty acids (a form of unsaturated essential fatty acid), said to have disease-countering benefits, are destroyed in the hydrogenation process.

Trans fats are commonly found in things you probably shouldn't be eating anyway: margarine, processed foods, fried foods, fast foods, and commercial baked goods such as cookies, cakes, and crackers.

Unsaturated Fat If double bonds are present in the fatty acid portion of the molecule, the fat is said to be unsaturated. If there is only one double bond present, it is called monounsaturated. If two or more double bonds are present, it is polyunsaturated.

Monounsaturated fats are considered to be the most healthful of all fats because they reduce LDL, which can cause blocked arteries. They are readily found in olive and canola oils, nuts, and seeds.

Polyunsaturated fats are more healthful than saturated or trans fats but not as healthful as monounsaturated fats because they lower both bad LDL and good HDL. But they do contain two very important essential fatty acids (EFAs) that cannot be synthesized in the body: omega-3 (alpha-linolenic acid) and omega-6 (linoleic acid).

Essential Fatty Acids Omega-6 fatty acids can be found in corn, sesame, safflower (unrefined), and sunflower oils. Omega-3 fatty acids can be found in linseed, flax, hemp, or soybean oil, pumpkin seeds, walnuts, or dark green vegetables. Both of these EFAs are necessary for good health. They regulate mental health, growth, and vitality, and assist in the transport and uptake of oxygen throughout the body.

PROTEIN

Although carbohydrates should be the foundation of your child's diet, with fat running a distant second, muscles need adequate protein. Used only minimally for fuel, protein's primary function is for building, maintaining, and repairing tissue and muscle.

Most athletes eat enough protein, and some even eat more than they need, believing it will help their performance. But contrary to popular opinion, muscle size is not dependent on protein intake. If daily minimum intakes are met, muscle size will be determined by the athlete's genetic potential first, then by the specific training demands.

Excess protein does, however, affect the body in other ways, typically leading to liver strain and kidney damage, calcium deficiency, and dehydration. Since protein cannot be stored for later use, extra protein will be broken down and either burned as carbohydrate or stored as fat.

High-protein foods should be avoided before and during training, because protein is the toughest nutrient to digest; a lot of energy is required to break it down.

Some examples of quality proteins are:

- Legumes

- Nuts

- Starchy vegetables (i.e., potatoes, corn, peas)

- Tofu

- Whole grains

Breads, cereals, and vegetables contribute small amounts of protein.

Overall, a high-carbohydrate diet is most important in ensuring optimal storage of carbohydrates in the body, fueling it for exercise, and supporting performance in your young athlete. In some people's minds, carbohydrates have a bad name, but this is because the term is often used to refer to refined junk foods and highly processed foods containing far too much simple sugar. For an athlete, young or old, the word *carbohydrate* should denote complex starches, mainly in their rough, unrefined forms with all their natural fiber and nutrients intact.

HOW MUCH DOES YOUR CHILD NEED TO EAT?

Since there are really no scientific data on the exact amounts of food a child needs for optimal health, the best way to estimate is by monitoring your child's weight and energy level.

If your child remains at a healthy weight even with the increased exercise of regular cycling, it's a good sign that the percentage increase in calories was correct. But if your child is showing signs of lethargy, it could be a signal to you to increase her calories. When doing so, put extra emphasis on high-quality carbohydrates, assuming that she is already eating the correct percentages of food as stated above.

SPECIAL ADVICE FOR OVERWEIGHT KIDS

Cycling can be a fun way for your child to burn off calories and shed pounds. Once she increases her exercise load, she may show an increase in body mass because her body will build muscle at a faster rate than it burns fat, and because muscle is actually heavier by volume. Good or bad, this is only temporary. Eventually, the fat-burning process will do its job to gradually take the weight off. As long as your child keeps with the program of exercising and a healthful diet, she'll reach her ideal weight.

If your child is gaining weight or if he is on his way to becoming overweight, you need to lower his caloric intake. First, try to identify any empty calories that can be eliminated such as his candy or soda habit; cyclists sometimes fall into the habit of eating bad food with the thought that it will all be burned off anyway. Once those items have been eliminated or reduced as much as you can, see if that does the trick.

If your child continues to gain weight, analyze his average diet to see how closely it matches the ratio of 60 to 70 percent carbohydrates, 20 to 30 percent fat, and 10 to 15 percent protein. If his diet fails to achieve this ratio, make an effort to reduce calories in a way that puts the percentages back in balance.

SPECIAL ADVICE FOR UNDERWEIGHT KIDS

With increased exercise comes increased calorie expenditure that needs to be replaced. Assuming that your kid is already eating the correct proportions of food, you may want to increase her overall daily caloric intake with emphasis on carbohydrates and healthful fats. The rule of thumb is to increase the carbohydrates first, since your child is active and will use the carbohydrates for energy as opposed to storing them as fat.

WHEN AND WHAT TO EAT AND DRINK

If your child has a big ride or race coming up, her nutritional preparation is essential to the success of the event. Proper nutrition may not be enough to guarantee a gold medal, but lack of the right fuel can ruin the day. It's not hard to believe that poor nutritional preparation has ruined more bike rides than all other culprits combined, except maybe the dreaded flat tire.

As long as you follow simple pre-event nutrition directions and use good food sense, your child will be prepared to enjoy the day to its fullest. Do keep in mind that your young rider should stick to foods that are tried and true; the day before or day of the big event is not the time to experiment with a new diet or food options.

THE NIGHT BEFORE A BIG EVENT

Feed your child a meal that's high in complex carbohydrates. By the time she wakes up, the carbohydrates will have been converted into glycogen, stored in muscles and ready for use. Some good choices:

Bowl of pasta with vegetables
Or
Grilled vegetables over rice
Or
Rice and bean burrito

Accompany any of these entrees with a salad, soup, and additional vegetable, fruit, and/or some bread. Also make sure your young rider drinks at least 2 to 4 cups of water the night before the ride.

IN THE HOURS BEFORE EXERCISE

Eating prior to exercise boosts blood sugar and prevents the needless fatigue associated with hypoglycemia (low blood sugar). Your child's preride meal should be very high in carbohydrates because they are most easily assimilated into energy. Some fat can be added to the meal as well, but protein should be kept at a minimum since it will not help the athlete to perform better—it slows down digestion and may contribute to dehydration.

The preride meal should be eaten 2 to 3 hours before your child gets on the bike. This allows time for her body to digest the food before her blood supply is focused toward her legs to pedal the bike. It is also okay to top off energy levels about 30 to 60 minutes before a ride with a light, carbohydrate-rich snack such as an energy bar or gel, fruit, or an energy drink.

As the length of the ride increases, so do the number of calories needed for preparation.

Here are some suggested meal options for different lengths of ride. The amount of food should be adjusted based on your child's age and specific needs. Also, the amount of liquid should be adjusted according to your child's age and the weather. On hot days, be sure to increase her fluid intake accordingly.

What to Eat and Drink 30 Minutes Before an Event

Preride Meal

Energy bar
 Or
High-carbohydrate drink
 Or
Piece of fruit (e.g., banana or apple)
 Or
Toast with jam

Fluid Intake

Up to one bottle of water or energy drink

Suggested Preride Meal Options for a 1-Hour Event

Fruit smoothie
 Or
Cereal with fruit
 Or
Toast with jam and banana
 Or
Energy bar and fruit

Fluid Intake

Up to one bottle of water or energy drink

Pancakes or waffles with syrup and juice or fruit
 Or
Peanut butter and jelly sandwich
 Or
Bowl of pasta
 Or
Two energy bars

Fluid Intake

Up to two bottles of water or energy drink

Large serving of pancakes or waffles with syrup and juice or fruit
 Or
Peanut butter and jelly sandwich, energy bar, and fruit
 Or
Big bowl of cereal with fruit and toast
 Or
Large serving of pasta

Fluid Intake

Up to two bottles of water or energy drink

Drinking

Your child needs to be completely hydrated well before he climbs onto his bike. By keeping his hydration levels high for the days leading up to the big event, his body will run more efficiently and will be better prepared to perform at its best.

Since the human body is made up of 60 to 75 percent water—and water is used by every cell of the body—H_2O is the foundation of all biochemical reactions and metabolic processes that take place in the body. Water aids in digestion and elimination of waste and provides a vehicle for transporting nutrients and oxygen throughout the body. It also lubricates joints, protects organs, and maintains normal body temperature.

For something this important, prevention is key. It is easier to prevent dehydration than to reverse its effects once it has occurred.

DURING THAT BIG RIDE OR RACE

When on the bike, the best nutritional advice to athletes of all ages is to eat before you're hungry and drink before you're thirsty. If a child waits for his body to tell her that it needs nourishment, the energy won't be able to reach her muscles fast enough to help. One nearly foolproof way to ensure that a rider will not exhaust her ready fuel supply is to set up a routine for eating and drinking. You can do this by setting your watch timer to go off every 20 minutes, so you can remind her to eat and drink. If she is riding on her own, send her off with instructions on how much to eat and drink every time her watch timer beeps.

Food

For the average 12-year-old boy weighing 100 pounds, the dietary requirements for an easy bike ride should be about 200 calories of food per hour. So, 200 calories is roughly equivalent to four Fig Newtons and an average energy bar, like a PowerBar. This figure will change depending on the sex of the child, the size of the child, the proportion of muscle mass, the intensity of effort on the bike, etc. Note that girls typically have less muscle mass per volume, so they need slightly fewer calories for the same effort.

If your child is larger than 100 pounds or if the intensity of the effort is greater than what is considered easy, then the calorie needs will also increase.

Food eaten on the bike should consist of readily available fuel for the effort; carbohydrates such as energy gel are the best. And since they digest at a more rapid rate than protein and fat, they are less likely to cause indigestion during your child's bike ride.

Snacks that are popular with kids are fruit such as bananas (rich in potassium—an important electrolyte for warding off muscle cramps), apples, cookies, fig bars, peanut butter and jelly sandwiches, and dried fruit (avoid citrus varieties, which can be hard on the stomach). Be sure to cut the food into bite-size pieces before putting it in plastic bags. This way, it will be easy for your child to eat.

As long as your junior athlete eats carbohydrate-heavy snacks almost continuously on long rides, he should be able to avoid the "bonk" (hypoglycemia). Identifying characteristics of the "bonk" include fatigue, dizziness, irritability, confusion, or nausea. Since blood glucose (circulating glycogen) is what fuels the brain and central nervous system, it is important to give your child's body the carbohydrates it needs for conversion into blood glucose.

Liquid

The same 12-year-old boy will also average about 24 ounces of liquid per hour, although this number will be altered depending on variables such as temperature, muscle mass, intensity of effort on the bike, etc. Since boys tend to sweat more than girls, they will consume slightly more water.

If your child is larger than 100 pounds or if the intensity of the effort is greater than what is considered easy, fluid levels will also need to increase.

On very hot days, be sure to increase your child's liquid intake. Keep in mind that a young athlete's exercise tolerance time will be shortened due to the heat, meaning that his fluid intake needs to be higher than normal. By freezing the water bottles the night before a ride, they will stay cooler longer and your young rider will be more likely to partake.

Eating food and drinking fluids with carbohydrates and electrolytes (sports drinks or juices) in addition to water is an easy way to reduce risks for hyponatremia, a dangerous dilution of blood plasma that can result from an excessive intake of plain water, on hot days and on long rides.

A fluid loss as small as one-half of 1 percent of bodyweight (i.e., 0.5 pounds in the case of a 100-pound child) can be enough to affect your child's athletic performance. If the fluid loss is more than 1 percent, he is considered to be dehydrated. Be on the lookout for signs of dehydration such as thirst, dry mouth, fatigue, irritability, and feeling hot. If any of these are apparent, increase your kid's liquid intake immediately.

If your child exhibits any outward signs of heat exhaustion such as nausea; dizziness; lethargy; or hot, red, or dry skin, get him into the shade right away. Lay him down and elevate his feet while loosening his clothing and helping him ingest more fluids. You can also cool your child down by misting cool water across his face and chest. If he has a fever or if fainting, confusion, or seizures occur, seek immediate medical attention.

To accurately monitor your child's fluid intake, weigh him before and after the ride. Most of his weight loss will be fluid; 1 pound of weight equals 2 cups (16 fluid ounces) of liquid. A weight loss signifies the need for a better hydration plan, but a stable weight suggests that your child is adequately hydrated.

POSTRIDE NUTRITION

Often overlooked, postride nutrition is important for replacing energy lost through exercise. It also aids in the repair of damaged and overworked muscles and in promoting growth. Proper postride nutrition also ensures rapid, healthful recovery, allowing your child to feel good and ride even better the following day(s). In order to maximize its effectiveness, recovery food must consist of high-quality nutrients and be eaten in a certain order at specified time intervals. The quantities of food and liquid will vary depending on various factors including age, weather, duration, and intensity of the event.

For instance, if your 12-year-old child went for a 30-minute easy ride, she may not need much nutritional recovery. But if it was scorching hot or she rode at maximum exertion during that time, a full nutritional recovery will be in order.

The Recovery Process

Within 10 Minutes after a Ride Your child should eat about 100 calories of simple sugars. This can come in the form of fruit, dried fruit, fruit drinks, energy drinks, a packet of gel, or something similar. She should also drink 2 to 4 cups of water or energy drink.

Within 30 Minutes after a Ride Your child should eat a small meal of 100 to 400 calories consisting of carbohydrate-heavy, easy-to-digest food such as bread, cereal, or sports bars.

Suggested Meals

Jelly sandwich
Granola bars
Fig bars
Dried fruit

Within 90 Minutes after the Ride Your child should drink one to two bottles of water.

Within 2 Hours after the Ride Your child should eat a large meal of 500 to 1,500 calories of mainly complex carbohydrates. This meal should also include lean protein, heart-healthy unsaturated fat, fruits, and vegetables.

Suggested Meals

Large bowl of pasta and veggies with bread and salad
Rice and bean burrito with chips, guacamole, and salsa

HELP YOUR KIDS CHOOSE A HEALTHFUL DIET

AT THE GROCERY STORE

You can steer your kids to choose a healthful diet by helping them to help themselves. When at the grocery store, let them be active participants in choosing food. As you go through the aisles, explain to your child what is going through your mind as you pick up one item and skip over another. Pick up each item and review its ingredients with your kid so he knows what to look for. What's fresh? What's ripe and tasty? What minerals or nutrients are in this or that?

Get your kid used to choosing nonpackaged foods. Most packaged foods contain a variety of chemicals, whether used for preservatives, taste enhancers, or fillers. Teach him how to identify those unwanted ingredients. Then show him how to avoid them by choosing whole, unprocessed foods whenever possible.

Take your child down the fruit and vegetable aisle and review each item, showing her how to choose the freshest or ripest of the bunch using our sensations of sight, touch, and smell.

Sad to say, many kids have never tasted fresh produce and eaten whole grains. Our modern, hectic lives remove us from contact with these healthful foods in the forms and rich flavors in which they emerge from the earth. One of the greatest gifts you can give your children is to renew that bond, so they can acquire lifelong affection for the foods that truly nourish us.

AT HOME

Be sure to have healthful snacks and easy-to-prepare foods on hand at home. This will prevent the postschool or postride binge on candy and potato chips. Some snacks that work well are fruit (both fresh and dried), baby carrots, peanut butter and jelly sandwiches, fig bars, and pretzels.

If busy parents are content to fulfill their obligation by handing over fattening, sugary packaged snack foods rather than taking the extra minute to slice an apple or wash some fresh vegetables, they shouldn't expect their children to develop sensible dietary habits. It takes a little more work, but the rewards are immense: healthy kids, with lean, active bodies, alert minds, and long, energetic lives ahead of them.

Kids will keep to the plan of eating healthful foods if you explain to them why proper nutrition is important and how it will allow them to have more fun on the bike. By eating a nutrition-packed diet, your child will have an increased level of energy, be stronger on the bike, and have sustained energy to enjoy herself for a longer period of time. A proper diet also ensures that she will recover quickly after rides and feel great the following day.

SUPPLEMENTS

If your child is eating a well-balanced diet, supplements are unnecessary. Misinformed parents may advise kids to take supplements in an

Since you are a role model for your kids, they will watch to see how you eat. Be sure to eat what you want them to eat. They will trust that what you tell them is true if they see you following your own nutritional guidelines.

....

effort to promote increased performance or as nutritional insurance. Yet, in some rare instances, nutritional deficiencies are the result of diseases or inherited conditions, and supplementation may be in order when directed by qualified health care professionals.

Supplements can give kids a false sense of security and may encourage faulty eating habits. Kids may assume that their morning dose of supplements provides them with all the nutrients that they need, so that they end up eating foods with low nutritional value.

With supplement use, your child may associate improvements in performance with whatever supplement he may be taking. He may be less likely to attribute progress to training, hard work, and a balanced diet—the factors that really make a difference. Supplements don't make up for lack of training or talent, and in certain cases they can be dangerous.

At the very least, supplements provide a template for a very dubious health practice: popping pills to take care of problems rather than addressing underlying conditions or ineffectual nutrition.

You can ensure that your child does not feel the need to use supplements by helping him feel confident about eating ordinary foods to achieve optimal performance.

AT THE END OF THE DAY

The best thing you can do for your child is to allow her to be an active participant in the fulfillment of her nutritional needs. The reason why most kids get involved in cycling is for freedom and control over their own lives. Just as your child enjoys steering the bike by herself while knowing how the bike works, she will enjoy knowing how nutrition affects her body and efforts on the bike. By knowing what, when, how, and why to eat, your young athlete will have the proper foundation for getting all she can out of cycling while leading a healthy, fulfilled life.

····················· **TRENT LOWE** ·····················

"When I was a small kid, I went riding with my dad once a week to the bakery. He would do it to keep fit and I would tag along. His father and uncle had also raced, so it was a family sport for me. Eventually, it was my brother who got me into mountain biking.

"Racing is addictive. You train hard every week so that you can do better at the races and then you do better and it just snowballs from there.

"'Garbage in, garbage out,' right? Nutrition is a big part of being a good rider. If you just have something that's full of sugar before you ride then after a few hours you'll be dead. So you need to eat something that will burn slowly and then keep eating so you don't go too far into the red zone.

"As a rough guide I know that I need to get through a bottle an hour. In the third or fourth day of a stage race you'll become depleted of minerals and you'll crave salt. Drinking sports drinks with the right amount of trace minerals and other hard-to-get elements that your body needs is important.

"Our team's leaders don't preach to us about how we should ride, they stay calm and make sure that everyone understands the plan for the race and then we go about getting it done.

"Certainly the majority of my friends I know through cycling. We have common interests and that's what pulls us together, but the people I spend the most time with also have other interests outside cycling and that helps keep them—and me—level."

··

PART VI

HOW TO BE A GREAT COACH

Being a Role Model Isn't Easy—
But It Is Rewarding

Although it may be too soon for structured practices that are appropriate for adult riders, in your outings with young riders you will be setting the tone that will shape their two-wheeled experience for a lifetime. Children will turn to you as their coach for intellectual guidance and emotional support. That gives you the power to make riding a positive learning experience that will inform their lives far beyond the bike. By providing them with fun, challenging experiences, you'll increase their confidence in their physical abilities and self-esteem.

At this stage, you're not the scowling figure of legend with the whistle and clipboard, steam blasting from your ears. Instead, you're the mentor, sometimes setting the example for how to receive helpful information, sometimes setting clear boundaries, but mostly just acting as a comforting ally. Even though society stresses the importance of winning and accomplishment, remember that the reason all of us hop on a bike is to have fun.

As with any relationship, coaching young cyclists will have its peaks and valleys. Sometimes you'll feel like your efforts have been wasted or ignored, but other times you'll feel as if you've succeeded far beyond your expectations. As long as you help your charges to set realistic goals—ones that are interesting to them—and give them the tools to achieve them, then you've taken the first, most important steps toward becoming a great coach.

BE A ROLE MODEL—SET AN EXAMPLE

Kids model much of their behavior after that of the adults close to them, and, in most cases, the adults they are around most are their parents. Children will learn more from your words and actions than they will from any other source. They will constantly look to you for cues. This is why it is incredibly important that you exemplify the kind of behavior that you want your kids to emulate. Your actions must always match your words. Kids learn how to approach sports by watching you. Your attitude toward children as well as toward officials, spectators, other parents, and your child's fellow competitors will be closely watched and should be of the highest standard. For example, if you want your kids to be good sports, you must be one, too. If you sulk and whine when things go wrong, why should you expect your children to be different? Kids will internalize your approach to all situations. Success is just one of those situations; how you respond to difficult challenges, stress, or failure is equally important. Your behavior in moments of adversity will remain vivid in your young rider's mind for a long time—long after you yourself have forgotten the incident.

IT'S NOT ABOUT YOU

Most adults who are nurturing young athletes had ambitions of their own when they were young. Maybe you were a first-string quarterback or an aspiring swimmer in high school. Perhaps you even had dreams of racing in the Tour de France. It could also be that you weren't good at sports when you were in school. Regardless of your background, it's not hard to believe that our early successes and frustrations may linger into our adult lives, and it's human nature to want to see the world through the lens of those achievements and missed chances.

Whatever the history or emotional investment may be, put it aside so that it doesn't cloud your efforts in helping a young rider both learn from cycling *and* find success. Your budding athlete has her own set of skills, ambitions, and distinct learning curve, and honoring that is paramount.

EMPHASIZE PROCESS OVER OUTCOME

In the adult world, it's readily accepted that winning isn't everything, it's the only thing. But that's not the case for young cyclists. Try to measure success in terms of effort, skills, improvement, and personal bests, not just the number of victories. By placing emphasis on these objects, you inspire the child to strive forward. At different developmental stages, the emphasis on various aspects of the process will change slightly. During your child's early years, there should be no emphasis on winning. As she reaches junior high and high school, she will naturally start becoming interested in crossing that finish line first, hands raised. That's fine, as long as it is self-inspired.

BE PATIENT

Kids think and learn like kids, and they all grow and absorb information at different rates. If your child needs an extra month to learn how to ride the bike without training wheels, give him time. Or if your child is not interested in riding his bike for a week, let him try something else. The more patience you offer your child, the more he will develop his own love for the sport. If he is on his own learning time line, he will master skills more rapidly instead of adopting simple survival strategies to placate you. Do you remember when you stayed up all night studying for that physics exam only to forget all the crucial equations by the end of the next week? The same concept applies with sports. It can be frustrating to the parent to simply sit back and wait, but the rewards are well worth it; your child will develop a more solid cycling foundation and love you for allowing him to develop in his own way and at his own pace.

JUNIOR ATHLETE GROWTH AND DEVELOPMENTAL PHASES

Although all kids grow and develop according to their own personal time line, many will follow a general progression of learning patterns and priority shifts in their athletics.

5 YEARS AND YOUNGER

During these years, it is important for your child to simply learn to enjoy riding a bike. The more she equates riding with positive experiences, the higher the probability that she will want to continue long after her formative years are past.

Most kids learn to ride a two-wheeled bicycle between the ages of 4 and 7. At this period in your child's life, her neuromuscular skills are developing rapidly. She is still learning to steady the bike, developing muscles to propel the bike forward, and even figuring out how to effectively stop the bike. You can serve your child best by focusing your efforts on teaching her the basics of riding a bike, including bicycle safety. Show your support by offering praise as often as possible. Acknowledge every effort she makes and every small accomplishment. For example, if she puts a lot of energy into riding the bike without training wheels, even if she hasn't succeeded yet, offer praise for her effort. Or if she learns how to make a U-turn, tell her how proud you are of her progress. It will mean a lot because it comes from you—the person she most wants to impress.

The other key to successfully coaching a very young child is an enormous amount of patience. Kids at this age are still coping with just *riding* a bike, so you can depend on them to make a lot of mistakes. It is okay to let your child repeatedly miss the mark.

Eventually, your child will succeed. What you can do that is best for your nerves and for your child's growth is to take a step back and give her the space to try over and over again until she gets it right. The lesson of "practice makes perfect" will serve you well as long as you allow your young one to progress at her own speed. It may be tempting to step in with pointed criticism, but if you allow her the opportunity to try different approaches, she will gain confidence at her own speed. She will see for herself how her mistakes and successes are related to the decisions she makes. Every time you intervene, do so very carefully, because you may risk blocking the connection that your child is making between her actions and the consequences of those actions.

6 TO 9 YEARS OLD

At this age, most kids have learned how to ride a two-wheeler. Assuming that there are positive experiences attached to the bicycle, they will start to develop a passion for riding. They may now start to experiment with playful competition, maybe challenging their buddies to race across the football field after school. It now becomes especially important, even more so than before, that you place emphasis on your child's effort and progress, rather than outcome. Acknowledge his work with lots of praise. The most he can ever ask of himself (and that you can ask of him) is to try his hardest.

Continue to show patience while your kid figures things out on his own. Only he knows when he's had enough of trying that wheelie or jumping off a curb. As long as you stay out of the way and allow him to experiment, he will do just that. And if he has had enough experimentation for the moment, he'll stop on his own. If he wants advice from you, he'll ask. It is better for your child to come to you for help than for you to offer it unsolicited; he knows that you are there for him.

10 TO 14 YEARS OLD

Assuming that your child has been riding a bike for a handful of years by this age, logging countless hours as he repeats various cycling tasks, he may be starting to show signs of real athletic talent. As he starts to get a general understanding of the sport, your praise for his mastery of various cycling skills will fuel his ambition—possibly inspiring him to take the sport to a higher level. It's at this age that a young rider may start to take interest in organized bike rides or races.

This is where the patience you have with your child will start to extend past allowing him room to grow; you will be responsible for moderating his tendency to put in too much time on the bike. Although his body is more developed, allowing him to handle more time on the bike at higher effort levels, he still has very distinct limits. "When we were kids, we'd watch the best guys and just assume that they went out and rode as hard as they could every day. It didn't take us long to figure out that wasn't a good way to train," says Discovery Channel Team Rider Tom Danielson. A young rider's body is not developed enough to assimilate arduous workloads without negative physical consequences. By keeping your child patient and teaching him how to read the signs of fatigue that his body sends out, you will keep him fresh and injury free.

This is a great age to start instilling a sense of real sportsmanship in your kids. As they learn the rules of the sport, they will come to understand proper behavior and become more accountable for their actions. It is your job to teach your children a sense of fair play and proper sportsmanship. There is a right way and a wrong way to react in any situation, whether difficult or easy. Poor sportsmanship can be displayed after winning a big race just as it can pop up after suffering a tough loss.

By the time your child reaches his teens, he is ready to take a more responsible stand in his commitment to himself and others. This becomes especially important if he wants to be part of a cycling club, possibly one affiliated with his junior high or high school. By joining a group, he is committing to do his share to ensure the smooth running of the club. This commitment includes showing up early for group events or letting others know well in advance if he will be unable to make a group function. Your child needs to be in charge of his commitment; if you manage his responsibilities for him, his development and understanding of team play will be constrained.

If you are certain that you have a highly talented athlete on your hands (and bear in mind, this is not easy to know for sure, since kids at this age are developing at wildly different rates), it is tempting to have him race against older or stronger kids. You may see this as good training for your young rider, but the truth is that often, this can do as much harm as good. While riding and racing with older, more developed riders will teach him an incredible amount, it may also demoralize him, as it's likely that he's not gifted enough to get the better of older competitors.

Guide your child carefully if he is considering a higher level of competition; he will no longer be the dominant kid, and at times he may finish near the back of the pack. There may also be added pressure to succeed if he jumps up a category too soon. This pressure can emanate from within your child or from peers, teammates, supporters, or family. If your child doesn't continue to win races in the more challenging category, he may become discouraged or lose faith in his abilities. Only he knows where his comfort level lies, but you can be there to help him make this and countless other crucial decisions.

15 TO 18 YEARS OLD

Now that your young athlete has reached her mid- to late teens, there may be a number of interests competing for her attention. When all her other surrounding references are placing emphasis on the outcome of her efforts, your role is to keep her focused on the process of proper training and preparation, putting it all together to help her achieve the best result.

Winning is always rewarding. However, it's important to learn that a victory is not an accident or a mysterious event. It is the product of many small, finite choices—a chain whose integrity is entirely dependent on the strength of its individual links. Real confidence comes from learning to trust the soundness of each smaller element, each link. As long as your young rider continues to build confidence this way, she will not be completely crushed or demoralized if she fails to win a big race. Crucially, she will see that any outcome—good or bad—can be a source of education.

During these years, a young rider's attention may be pulled in various directions, such as dating, friends, cars, shopping, and other sports or interests. In a way, these distractions serve as a vetting process for those who feel that their talents or interests lie elsewhere. They may help your child decide on his own whether he wants to continue to cycle regularly or compete in bike races at all. If your child shows "middle of the pack" talent but clearly enjoys the sport anyway, then your job is to continue to provide lots of positive feedback. The most important thing is for him to continue to exercise. And you never know, he may just be the next Lance Armstrong with time to develop and continued encouragement.

Keep in mind that puberty affects each child differently; a chubby child may grow long and lean, while a skinny kid may become chubby. An apparently athletically mediocre child may turn into a superstar, while young hotshots might fall by the wayside. By supporting your child and acting "as if" she is succeeding with every effort, you will give her every opportunity to do just that.

If your child has reached 15 years of age and is determined to be the best he can be in cycling, the next logical step is to have his skills finely tuned by an expert—a certified professional cycling coach. When searching for a coach, look for someone who is certified by cycling's governing body, USA Cycling, and who has solid experience with junior athletes. Any child in this age group is still growing at an astonishing rate. These next few years will lay the groundwork for the rest of his cycling career and athletic life.

NO TWO KIDS PROGRESS AT THE SAME RATE

Although most kids fall under loosely defined progression guidelines, it's been proven best to let your child follow his own rate of progression. Genetics, environment, and other factors will affect your child's athletic development. Maybe he is the younger brother of an elite cyclist or the son of a pro cyclist and grew up with cycling all around. He may know the names of all the bike parts and some cycling rules, and maybe he's even mastered various cycling skills faster than his peers, but he is still a growing child and he needs to do this at his own rate. Discovery Channel Team's George Hincapie, the only rider to race with Lance Armstrong in all seven of his Tour de France victories, didn't win every race he entered when he was just starting out. But his father, a lifelong cyclist, believed in supporting him and allowing him to progress at his own rate. Now he is acknowledged as one of the greatest riders in the world. "I rode on a bike path and in a park near my home in Queens, New York, for a long time before I was ready to race," says Hincapie. "That base of development really allowed me to be better once I started racing."

KIDS' MENTAL ABILITIES ALSO MATURE AT VARYING RATES

The level at which your child learns has limited, if any, bearing on her long-term success as a cyclist. One child may learn how to ride a bike at 3 years old, while another may not learn until the age of 7. Lance Armstrong didn't learn how to ride a bike until he was 5 years old, but he turned out to be one of the finest cyclists who ever lived.

KIDS' BODIES ARE STILL GROWING

A child's bones are not as strong as an adult's for the simple reason that they are still growing. The growth plates at each end of the bone are weaker than the ligaments (connecting one bone to the next) and tendons (connecting muscle to bone) that tie them together. Since ligaments and tendons don't grow as fast as bones during growth spurts, your child may experience limited flexibility. This imbalance can lead to injury if she is not careful. She may seem to recover quickly, but too much long and/or hard cycling can actually get in the way of a young rider's ability to heal and grow. Overuse is the most common physical problem for young athletes—more common than injuries or even accidents.

Overuse problems are easy to spot and correct, if caught early enough. There are clear warning signals to look out for. The biggest one is pain. The old adage, "No pain, no gain" is just that—old and outdated. The new one that you and your child must take heed of is, "Stop if it hurts." Be aware that your child may ignore a subtle, lingering pain, thinking that it's all part of the sport. He may even hide it because "the big ride" is just around the corner. But he needs to be aware that if this little ache is not nipped in the bud, there may not be another big ride for a long time to come. It's more than possible that this once subtle annoyance could turn into a full-blown health issue, requiring months or possibly years to correct. Kids tend to want to play their favorite sport no matter what the cost. If your junior athlete insists on playing through the pain, you need to say no, or at the very least have the trouble examined by a trained medical practitioner. If the pain persists, find another doctor, one well-versed in sports injuries common to children.

Just as overuse can injure your child's body, overexposure can kill his enthusiasm for and interest in the sport. He can become a classic victim of burnout. Your job as the coach is to keep your child feeling fresh, both physically and mentally. The more a child focuses on cycling at the expense of everything else in his life, the greater the chances for burnout. As a young cyclist strives to be the best he can be, he may start to ignore other important areas in his young life such as school, family, or social activities. Even though cycling may be a healthful activity for your child, too much of a good thing is simply too much. Signs of burnout include reduced physical capabilities, an inability to concentrate, or complaints of being constantly tired.

To counteract burnout, respond immediately. First, try talking to your child to pinpoint the actual cause. Very often, the answer is too much stress. Start by letting him know that his situation is normal and that it's okay to take time to step back and decide on the right level of commitment to cycling. This will ensure that every time he rides, it's because he's decided he wants to. Next, help him deal with any noticeable stress that is related to cycling. This can be as simple as helping him clarify his thoughts on a recent challenge or situation where he may have felt overwhelmed. Praise for every small progression is of utmost importance if you suspect that your child is on the express train to burnout. The cues he gets from you will give him the motivation to believe in his abilities while focusing on the process, rather than on the outcome. Finally, emphasize the need to have fun.

BASIC STEPS TO DEVELOPING YOUR JUNIOR ATHLETE'S CYCLING SKILLS

Before your child can begin to master a skill, she must first be taught about it. As the coach, you must fully comprehend the task at hand so that you can explain it to her clearly. As long as she understands what the skill is, why it is important, and how best to execute it, you will have the greatest chance for success. For example, if you are trying to teach her how to ride without training wheels, you will need to convince her that once she is without the outrigger wheels, it will be easier to ride and that, eventually, she will have more balance and freedom and better turning ability.

This step is particularly poignant because it will lay the groundwork for any and all of her future growth as a cyclist. Each step of this kind reinforces a critical aspect of learning: Our anxiety about something we haven't tried is often unwarranted, and the new skill often turns out to be much, much easier than we had imagined. By mastering simple, small-scale fundamentals, your child will be a better, safer cyclist and will have the building blocks to learn more advanced skills. In turn, these good skill-building habits will build her self-esteem and can be applied to other areas of her life, helping her to succeed outside of cycling as well.

Second, your child has to perform the skill repeatedly. This kind of repetitive motion will imprint both the mind and the body's memory. Although this step is crucial in nailing a skill, it does take lots of time and constant feedback. The problem is, repetition is inherently boring. That's where the coach-as-motivator comes in. You play an important role in making the repetitive process fun. Come up with games to keep your child's interest in learning this new skill. For instance, if you are teaching your fledgling cyclist how to lean into a turn, take her to a playground or empty parking lot, draw a wide circle (a trick is to fill a water bottle with white baking flour and "squirt" marks, lines, or circles from the opened nozzle), and play "catch me if you can." You and your child start on opposite sides of the circle, riding in the same direction. When one of you almost catches the other, announce—or have your child announce—a U-turn, so that you're now chasing each other in the opposite direction. Or maybe when teaching your child to track-stand during a ride (balancing without moving forward), see who can come closest to each stop sign without having to put a foot down. Keep score, and whoever wins by the end of the ride is absolved of doing dishes that night. Or maybe if she wins, you take her out for dessert after the ride.

Third, your child now has to work on executing the learned skills, but this time without thinking about it. Assuming that the first two steps were carried out successfully, the third will be easy. Your child has to feel the learned action and commit it to muscle memory, not calculate it. As Yogi Berra once stated about hitting a baseball, "You can't think and hit at the same time." Your child must trust that the skill will be automatic, so when it is needed, the resource will be there with no advance notice required. You can support your child by reminding her to trust in herself; she has done the necessary work to learn the skill.

GOAL SETTING

As with adults, goals play an important role in children's lives. They can help to motivate a child, getting him to focus on the task at hand while putting persistent effort into it. They are also effective in developing new learning strategies. Each time a goal is achieved, it builds self-confidence. Cycling can be a great forum for your young athlete to learn proper goal setting. "A lot of what I've learned from cycling has nothing to do with winning races, and I can carry that into my life beyond cycling," says Tom Danielson of the Discovery Channel

"In October, after you've been riding the whole year, you think you're sick of it. But, you take a month off and suddenly you've got the feeling for it back, you can't wait to suffer for a few hours and be hungry enough to eat a good dinner.

"Once I started racing as a professional, I realized there was another level in terms of fitness and skills and suppleness. It forced me to raise my level.

"Being a great racer isn't something you can just see on a video and go out and do it. Actually doing that is the only way to become as good as you can be.

"Johan (Bruyneel) and Lance (Armstrong) said to me, 'Tom, you need to learn to ride more in the saddle.' So, I would do workouts where Johan would ride behind me in the car, beeping every time I stood up. It takes discipline to change your riding style like that, but it helped me more than anything I've probably ever done.

"As a kid I tried to ride 30 hours a week, as hard as I could, and I got strong but I also got really tired. It's not how much you train, it's how efficiently and smart you train. You've got to keep things in check. Make sure that you're building. You want to break it down a little, but you also want to finish with something in the tank so you can go out the next day.

"My wife is a pro mountain bike racer, so we share that common ground. Cycling is part of why I love her and it's part of what makes us a great team."

Team. "For example, working together and getting along in an organization where there are a lot of different kinds of people is an amazing skill to learn."

To get the most out of the goal-setting process, your child must play an active role in choosing the targets, determining the plan of action to realize them and the time it will take. If you include your young rider in the goal-setting process, he will intuitively understand expectations and will show a deeper commitment to nailing the goal. Once he has achieved success a few times, he'll learn an important lesson:

that life is little more than a series of goals, and success is predictable if you follow the right process.

Choosing an Appropriate Goal

There is an incredible range of goals that you and your child can set. There are subjective goals, such as feeling more comfortable riding in the drops of the handlebars. And there are objective goals, such as mastering a certain technical singletrack trail without dabbing (touching a foot to the ground for balance) or taking a minute off a "personal best" time on a given course. The goal chosen should always be in the positive mode: Emphasize *what to do*, not what to *stop* doing.

Most young athletes have goals of some sort already floating around in their heads. As your child's guide, you need to coax those goals from him. If his thinking is lofty, possibly requiring years of effort, then help him to break this ultimate goal into smaller goals that will lead to success in the main goal. For instance, if he wants to be Road Race World Champion (a goal that Lance Armstrong set for himself as an adolescent), you might help him to create a succession of smaller, more tangible goals that can be achieved along the way. For instance, have him focus on a possible weak point in his cycling. Or begin with knocking 30 seconds off the time it usually takes him to ride up the local climb. Next, focus on winning a race on a regional scale. After that, his goal could be to improve his descending skills. And the following goal could be to become Junior State Champion. Each of these smaller goals should have its own deadline and plan of action. It's important in each instance that the athlete be able to see the way in which a goal follows naturally from good habits and decisions and discipline, not from merely hoping or wishing. He needs to understand that the outcome is something he has control over and that it is repetitive if the right steps are followed.

SET A DEADLINE

Once a goal or series of goals has been defined, a time line or deadline must be set. It should be one that makes the task attainable yet still challenging. Have your child set the deadline on her own. This will give her the chance to think it through, balancing the difficulty of the task with how much time she is willing or able to dedicate to achieving it. If she chooses a deadline that seems either too short or too long, make sure she understands the range of factors that can affect a drive toward a goal. In the end, you should arrive at a time line that you both think is fair.

DETERMINE THE PLAN OF ACTION

You have a goal and a deadline. Now is the time to fill in the details. Ask your young rider how he plans to reach his goal—what his steps are. You can give him subtle coaching and even overt advice, but don't insist that yours is the only way. It is your job to help him think the process through and offer advice when he needs help.

Once the child is working toward his chosen goal, it is the coach's job to provide continuous feedback and positive reinforcement, motivating the rider to achieve his goal. If it looks like he may not be on track, talk to him about it. Ask what he thinks about his plan of action and how it may need to be adjusted. It's likely that he will agree with you that a redefinition of the goal is in order. Either a new time line or a new end point needs to be chosen. It is fine to set a few goals at a time, but be sure they are clear and prioritized and that they don't overwhelm your young rider. This could lead to low motivation and burnout.

SHOW SUPPORT AND ENCOURAGEMENT

Kids are great at motivating themselves; the more fun they have, the more they will play. Most often what your child needs from you is not motivation, but answers to her questions and positive reinforcement. With your support, she has the opportunity to perform well beyond her level of natural talent simply because she believed she could. As coach and parent, you can show support in a vast number of ways. Think about your own career. When are you most productive and satisfied? How motivated are you when all you're doing is following someone's instructions and not chasing after a big goal? To feel that you're in charge makes a huge difference, and kids are no different in that regard.

Listen More Than You Talk Ask questions that prompt thought. Since we have to know what our children's opinions and feelings are before we can do anything about them, good questions are more important than good answers. They open the door to meaningful communication to help kids focus on issues that are or should be important to them. Listeners are learners, and learners are winners. By being a good listener, you are learning about your child to better help her succeed. You are also helping her to be a good listener since you are her role model. By asking incisive questions, you can encourage reflective thinking, and children who can self-reflect make good decisions.

Treat Your Child with Respect Kids respond well when talked to in a respectful manner. You will have an easier time communicating valuable information, and the chances that your athlete will take it in are much higher. In stressful moments, it is especially important that you stay calm and that your words and actions are well chosen. When you were young, coaches commonly yelled at and berated their athletes. Think about how you felt when you were screamed at in front of a large crowd or a class of your peers. Yelling makes a child feel worthless, and children who feel worthless do not follow instruction and quickly lose interest in the activity. For that reason, many of the old-school coaching techniques such as shouting, belittling, and punishing have fallen by the wayside. Great coaches are now using the approaches of listening, looking, and then explaining, in that order.

CRITICIZE USING A "COMPLIMENT SANDWICH"

There may be times when you need to criticize your child. There are good times and preferable ways to do this. It is always easier for a child to accept criticism when he is in good spirits, such as after winning a race or returning from a fabulous bike ride. The time *not* to criticize is when he is feeling frustrated, agitated, sad, or tired. Anything you say during those moments will, at best, go in one ear and out the other. At worst, it will blow his negative feelings out of proportion, possibly leading to depression or to wanting to hang up the bike for good.

When dishing out criticism, follow the proven technique of the "compliment sandwich." First, give your child a compliment, then criticize, and immediately follow up with a compliment. For example, if he has just done well in a race, tell him how proud you are that he rode a really smart race, incorporating all the skills that he's recently learned. Then tell him that he needs to be more gracious on the podium—don't push the second- and third-place riders off the podium while climbing up to the top step, for example. Finally, tell him that you noticed his improvement on the technical descents.

Acknowledge and Praise Every Small Progression When children are very young, their primary focus every time they get on the bike is to have fun. There is no deeper thought than this. As they get older, their focus is still on fun, but they start to care about improving their skills and getting stronger on the bike. As long as they see progress—confirmed by your continuous acknowledgment and praise—they will feel successful and strive for more positive feedback.

Share Your Child's Love for Cycling Chances are high that *you* are the very reason your child became interested in the sport. The benefit of sharing in the sport with your child is that it gives you something that you can do together to help strengthen your bond. Your kid will also come to you for advice and support when he needs it; your words will mean more to him because you understand his world.

DEALING WITH FRUSTRATION

Frustration is the internal reaction that kids often have when they cannot do something correctly or get what they want. It is the biggest reason why kids quit sports. Since it is no fun to be frustrated, kids will often try to quit simply to rid themselves of that awful feeling. Your junior cyclist needs to understand that frustration is common in sports; it is not only normal but also part of the process that leads to success.

If your child is clearly frustrated, try to get her to identify the cause. Reassure her that it is perfectly normal to find frustration in sports or in anything else with a big payoff. Then get her to tell you in specific terms what she finds frustrating. Assuming that the situation or challenge isn't too much for your child to handle, help her to come up with a game plan. Sometimes all your child needs is a break from the activity. Give her permission to take a step back. Never push beyond her own inclination to address the problem. If she strongly resists your input, drop the subject. With time, her own natural love of cycling will bring her back to the issue that needs attention or resolution.

Frustration in itself is not bad, but not being able to cope with it is. Children who persist until they get it right learn how to effectively manage frustration. They will have better experiences in their cycling and be able to apply those skills to other areas of their lives.

DEALING WITH ANXIETY OR FEAR

Help your child to come up with a positive mantra, a mental ritual, for when she is nervous. It should be something simple like, "I can do this" or "I just need to do my best." You can also teach your child to talk back to negative thoughts. For instance, if your child is thinking, "I'm going to fail," then encourage her to tell herself, "I've worked hard for this moment. I'm prepared to do my best." If this is challenging for your junior athlete, have her talk to herself in the same way she would encourage a friend or teammate. Sometimes it's easier for kids to envision talking back to fear in this way.

DEALING WITH DISAPPOINTMENT

Disappointment can be turned around with support from a loving parent. Young riders don't want to hear, "You win some, you lose some." What they want to hear is, "That really stinks." Sometimes all they need is validation of their disappointment and frustration. You may also add, "Let's see if we can figure out how to turn this around next time." You can share a personal experience in which you were disappointed. Explain how you handled that situation so that it led to a positive outcome. Kids learn from unsuccessful attempts, turning them into triumphs by trial and error. They're no different from adults in that respect. By supporting them and offering encouragement, you can motivate them to try again.

KEEPING IT FUN

Just like you, the main reason why your child rides a bike is to have fun. It should mainly be play, expressing physical pleasure and joy. Never take that away from a young rider. If a child expects to have fun and doesn't, the experience wasn't successful. Of secondary importance to a child is playing with friends, improving fitness, and learning new skills. Parents also want these goals for their kids, along with a variety of other benefits such as sportsmanship, critical evaluation, self-discipline, integrity, and self-esteem. As long as the sport

If you keep riding fun, kids will likely ride more often.

remains fun for children, they will continue to play. The more your child plays, the more you will both get what you want out of the sport.

Think Like a Child Parents are best with kids when they are in their most childlike state. What you wanted from your parents is what your child wants from you. She wants simple, straightforward instruction. It is most effective because it doesn't taint her euphoria with a parental agenda or moralizing. Riding a bike should mean just that— no deeper meaning. Once you get into defining what a bike ride should mean to a child or what it means to take off the training wheels, your child will become bored and start to see the bike as less than fun. Famed child psychologist Jean Piaget said that play is the business of childhood. And the more fun it is, the more your child is likely to learn. This is the key to turning cycling into a sport for a lifetime.

Kids Ride Bikes for Freedom By giving kids the freedom they want, cycling sets the tone for how they will live life on a larger scale. Can you remember how it felt the first time you rode away from your yard and your neighborhood, beyond the grasp of adults? Kids use bikes as a means of escape—on many occasions, to escape from you! It's healthy, it's part of growing up, and it's an exhilarating experience for all children who are *permitted* to feel it. A little freedom helps kids fuel their ambitions and define their sense of themselves in the world. We as parents must know when to stand aside. That's what great coaches do: They impart the skills, the discipline, and the mental tools, and then release their athletes into the world.

....

PART VII

CYCLISTS FOR LIFE

*How to Keep Cycling Long
After Anyone Calls You a Kid*

....

Life, as John Lennon said, "is what happens to you while you're busy making other plans." As it turns out, those plans often distract you from riding a bike. The distraction can take hold in your teen and college years, when any number of extracurricular activities are likely to pull you away from your favorite ride, and persist through your late twenties, when building a career and starting a family assume central importance, into the years of middle age, when your body slowly begins to betray you.

If you intend to keep on cycling into your golden years and you want your kids to do the same, you'll need to anticipate the challenges that life and physiology will throw at your entire family. Following are strategies for overcoming the bogies that are most likely to derail your and your child's time on two wheels.

THE TEENS

The teenage years are so full of distractions, from pressure for good grades to the desire for a driver's license, that there are any number of perfectly valid reasons why a child who grew up riding and loving cycling might quickly forget its fun and adventure. "When I was in school, cycling wasn't an option for me to pursue seriously," says Discovery Channel Team rider Roger Hammond of the United Kingdom. "There was too much pressure to play rugby or soccer." And who can blame kids for wanting to experience everything possible while they're young? Chances are that, if they've had fun riding as children, they've caught the "bug" and the basic skills that will pull them back to the bike at some point. Here are a few tips to keep your child riding through the distraction-filled years of high school and college.

······················ ROGER HAMMOND ·······················

"I did my first race at age 8; it was cyclocross. You had to be 12 years of age to ride on the road, but for cross you could be younger.

"My dad was brought up in a cycling family and, thanks to him, I was brought up in a cycling environment.

"Most of my long-term friends are cyclists. The beauty of cycling is that it's a family, it's a big community.

"One of the great beauties of cycling is that, if you put in the effort and dedication, 9 times out of 10 you get the result you're looking for.

"When it's really horrible weather I do some type of training that's more pleasant. I go off-road and do two hours in the woods. It's not miserable. I find a way to suit the conditions more. For a given day of training, you've got a certain amount of work to do and if it's pleasant you'll do it better.

"The feeling of coming home after achieving something feels good. That's the pleasure I gain from cycling.

"Cycling is just like school. If you have the pressure to do something, and you are able to think of the end result, that makes it very simple. At the end of the day, training never goes away. The quicker you get out, the quicker you get home and the quicker you're in the bath."

EQUIP THEM

High school and college students aren't known for their discretionary income; buying a few boxes of macaroni and cheese always takes precedent over picking up a spare tube. So make sure your child has all the equipment she needs to get out on two wheels. A care package of the bike's most expendable parts—tubes, tires, chains, lube, etc.— can go a long way toward making it easy for a student to keep her bike in good riding condition.

INSPIRE THEM

Take your kids to new places to ride, include cycling in your next vacation, and consider sending them to a summer camp that has riding as the central focus. During a child's teen years, it's more important than ever before that cycling intermingles at least in part with his social landscape. In recent years, freeride and mountain bike camps that cater specifically to teens and younger children have gained an immense amount of popularity. Woodward Camp (www.woodwardcamp.com), which has three locations, and Whistler Blackcomb resort (www.whistlerblackcomb.com), north of Vancouver, British Columbia, are two of the most reputable freeride and mountain bike camps.

INFORM THEM

Without being preachy, let your kids know the health, ecological, and social benefits of riding bicycles:

- According to *Scientific American* magazine, the average person worldwide spends 66 minutes per day traveling, yet less than 10 percent of all Americans get the required amount of exercise per day. Riding a bicycle has not been shown to significantly increase travel time, and it burns roughly 500 calories per hour.

- The AMA says that just 20 minutes of exercise such as cycling three times per week is enough to help ward off America's most common ills, including obesity, heart disease, and hypertension.

- The average cost of owning and operating a car is $6,150 more per year than owning and operating a bicycle. Also, 80 percent of all trips by car are less than 1 mile; 90 percent are less than 2 miles.

MAKE IT EASY FOR THEM

When it comes right down to it, you won't ride a bike if it's not just as easy as hopping into a car and turning the key. So, it's important for your young adults to have an inexpensive city bike complete with fenders, lights, and some kind of rack. A bike that's easy, comfortable to ride, and incredibly dependable will make walking or driving a car less attractive options.

THE TWENTIES

Because the sole purpose of most humans for most of human history has been simply to raise their offspring to the age of independence, the average life expectancy has not been much over 20 years. The best way to be sure that you and your kids beat Mother Nature's calendar is to start thinking about your long-term health early in the game.

KEEP THE WEIGHT OFF

At some point in their twenties, most people realize that they just can't eat the way they used to without stacking on some additional pounds. The obvious way to avoid the extra weight is to eat healthful food in reasonable quantities and to ride regularly. One good way to see the effects of your riding is to ride with a powermeter such as those from SRM and Powertap. These devices can tell you exactly how many calories you've burned during the course of a ride. "Not only does a powermeter let you know exactly how much energy you're using, but it tells you how tired your body is; it keeps you from training too hard," says Discovery Channel Team rider Michael Barry.

STRETCH TO LIVE

You'll begin losing flexibility at an increasingly rapid rate. That can cause problems from your neck to your back and down to your knees, but stretching just a few times a week for 15 to 30 minutes can significantly improve bloodflow to all parts of your body and decrease the chance of injury. "In addition to knowing exactly how hard to ride based on my fitness, I know that stretching every day is incredibly important," says Discovery Channel Team rider Michael Barry. "If you stretch and progress slowly in your training, you'll have much less of a chance of getting injured." Develop a stretching routine when you're in your twenties and encourage your children to stretch, too. You'll all feel better for life.

BUILD STRENGTH NOW

Thanks to high amounts of human growth hormone and testosterone, humans reach peak muscle mass sometime between the ages of 18 and 25, making this the best time of life to build and strengthen the muscles that will carry you through the next 60 to 80 years. "I spend a lot of time in the gym over the winter just working on my core strength," says Discovery Channel Team rider George Hincapie. "Just by doing some basic stretches and exercises like situps and back extensions, I can feel that I'm more comfortable and relaxed when I'm sitting on the bike."

THE THIRTIES

If you didn't get married, buy a home, and have kids in your twenties, there's a good chance that you'll do one or more of those things in the decade that follows. In any case, you'll find that your time and energy are under ever-increasing pressure. If you want to hit the big four-o riding comfortably and feeling healthy, you'll need to anticipate and battle a few physical changes.

BE HEART SMART

In your early thirties, you'll see the strength and endurance of your heart peak. Like any other muscle in your body, it will continue to lose strength and stamina as you grow older. At the same time, fatty deposits will build on the walls of the arteries that surround the heart, while cholesterol mounts and blood pressure rises. Keep in

(continued on page 133)

"When I was younger, I didn't know how hard I needed to push myself or when to take it easy. Probably the biggest mistake that most riders make when they don't have experience is that they train too hard on their hard days and not easy enough on their easy days.

"Now that I've been racing for a long time, I really notice that when I don't stretch I get way more aches and pains. Stretching is a huge help for me; it's an amazing way to keep healthy and fit.

"In the off-season I do a lot of work on my core strength. I go into the gym a few times a week and do situps and lower back extensions. I also do Pilates to help build my core muscles."

front of this potential problem by eating a diet low in saturated fats, riding regularly to keep your heart strong. Most important, see your doctor for regular checkups. It doesn't matter how fit you are or how great you feel; if you are congenitally predetermined for heart disease, you may have a high risk.

CUT CALORIES

As you grow older, your metabolism slows predictably. Some experts say the average person requires about 12 calories less per day per year over 20. So, at 40, you need 120 fewer calories per day just to maintain bodyweight. Combine that with the fact that you are naturally less physically active as you grow older, and you absolutely have to adjust your eating habits as you age if you want to maintain a similar body mass.

SAY YES TO YOGA

The older you get, the more strength and flexibility you lose in your tendons and joints. That makes riding, which is very low-impact, great for bodies even as they grow older. Yet cycling alone isn't enough to help you maintain balance, strength, and flexibility. Consider taking up yoga; just two or three hour-long sessions per week will help you counteract the effects of Father Time on your joints and tendons.

THE FORTIES

Fifty, as people have become fond of saying lately, may be the new 40, but 40 is still a physical landmark to be reckoned with. Fortunately, at this point you should know your body better and understand how it reacts to physical activity. And, if you're like most people, you'll have a little more time to work out.

SLOW THE SHRINKAGE

Once past the age of 40, your bones, muscles, and connective tissue will begin to shrink. There's not a complete method for stopping this natural process, but with the right steps, you can slow or minimize their effects. One of the best things you can do is to strengthen your abs and lower back. That will help you maintain proper posture and support your spine.

WARM UP TO IT

Because you're slowly becoming a little more creaky, it's important that you get a good warmup before you make a hard effort on the bike. Warming up actually elevates your body's temperature, making your muscles more elastic and lessening the chance of injury. It also stimulates the flow of your joints' natural lubricant.

SWEAT OFF THE BIKE

Because you are slowly losing muscle, it's more important than ever that you keep the muscle that you have as strong and fit as you can. If possible, you also want to add new muscle mass while cutting fat. Gain just 1 pound of muscle and you burn an additional 50 calories every day! You can do all this by hitting the gym for as little as 30 minutes twice per week. Find a complete workout that will exercise your entire body, including your shoulders, arms, and neck.

THE FIFTIES

You may have deluded yourself to this point, but there's no denying that when you hit 50, you're going to feel the effects of aging. Sure, you might not be "old," but there are a number of physical changes that you have to account for if you want to keep riding long and strong.

CHUG-A-LUG

The body of a young, healthy person is composed of 61 percent water, but as you grow older, you slowly start to dry out. In your late fifties, your body can be as little as 54 percent H_2O. Add to that the fact that your sensation of thirst decreases with age, so that you're less likely to want to drink. The key? Drink early and often. Drink off the bike, drink on the bike. Drink until you're full and then drink more. Awareness is half the battle; heading out for a ride with a full hydration pack is the other.

BONE UP

Once past the age of 35, you begin to lose bone mass, and once you're into your fifties, that loss can begin to be noticeable. Fortunately, there are a number of things you can do to counteract bone loss. First, start taking calcium supplements—the average 50-year-old needs about 1,200 milligrams of calcium per day to maintain healthy bones.

RIDE A BIKE

Men in their fifties are more likely to experience trouble with their joints than at any age up to that point. The good news is that riding just 25 minutes, three times per week was found by researchers to lessen pain and increase physical well-being in everyday life.

BEYOND YOUR FIFTIES

By the time you hit your sixth decade, the battle against aging is in full gear. Many of the changes that people have traditionally considered simply effects of aging are actually the result of environment, disease, or diet—so you can minimize them if not eliminate them completely.

NEVER TOO LATE

The physical effects of more than 60 years of battling gravity and the elements will become apparent, as your skin will become thinner and less elastic. Even if you haven't been a big user of sunscreen yet, it's never too late to begin. Wear 30 SPF sunscreen on every outing—even when it's foggy or gray—and focus on your most exposed parts, especially your nose, your lips, and the tops of your ears.

MUSCLE MISSED

The trend of muscle depletion that started sometime in your late thirties is in full swing as you blow past 60. As shown previously, there are ways to battle the loss of muscle mass. Spend more time in the gym or in yoga classes, focusing on your core strength but also working your arms, neck, and shoulders. Yoga is a particularly low-impact method of building muscle while increasing the flexibility of muscles and joints.

KEEP YOUR RESPONSES STRONG

As you age, your body's response time will slow. You can minimize the amount of slowdown by doing workouts and playing games that keep your responses sharp. This includes anything from playing Ping-Pong to shooting basketball and even playing video games.

IS THERE A DOCTOR IN THE HOUSE?

There's no question that all seniors need to visit their physician more frequently the older they get. If you are trying new types of workouts (switching from yoga to tai chi, for example) or anticipating a new challenge on a bicycle, ask your doctor for an opinion. Chances are, he or she will have some advice to help you feel better and live longer.

IF YOU WANT TO GET OUT MORE, GET ORGANIZED

In the space of a decade, many people go from worrying about their midterm college finals and what to wear out on a Friday to having a serious career, getting married, owning a home, and having children of their own. Needless to say, the 2-hour weekday and 3- to 5-hour weekend rides that were a mainstay of their teen years begin to become less and less frequent. So, the secret as you ease into adulthood is to develop increasingly more efficient coping strategies to ensure that every ride is a great ride—because whether it's getting out the door or out on the road, there's no longer any time to waste. Here are seven tips for helping you make the most of every single ride.

1. KEEP YOUR BIKE READY

Many times, the difference between getting out for a ride or not lies in the details of having your bike and equipment organized and ready to roll. Where your bike is concerned, make sure the tires are inflated, the water bottle is filled, and the drivetrain and brakes are in good working order.

2. STAY GEARED UP

Having your bike ready to roll is only half the battle; organizing the clothing and other equipment that you'll need to ride is every bit as important. Dedicate a small space to storing and organizing your gear, and make sure that everything you need to get out the door is collected in this area. This includes a helmet, jerseys, jackets, shorts, knee and arm warmers, gloves, socks, shoes, a heart rate monitor, spare tubes, mini-tools, a hand pump or CO_2, glasses, energy bars, and anything else you might need for an average ride. It's best to

The best way to stoke your fire for riding even if you've been riding for decades is to set new goals and take on new challenges. This can be as simple as trying a type of cycling that you've never given much thought to, setting a goal to beat your best time up a local climb, or planning a trip to ride in a foreign country. Here are some resources to help you find and conquer your next big challenge.

THE ADVENTURE CYCLING ASSOCIATION With a mission to inspire people to travel by bicycle for fitness, fun, and self-discovery, this Missoula, Montana–based firm provides fully guided tours to maps and everything that you could ever need to find an amazing two-wheeled adventure. Visit www.adv-cycling.org.

CARMICHAEL TRAINING SYSTEMS Founded by the coach who helped Lance Armstrong win seven consecutive Tours de France, CTS has a range of programs and camps that will help sharpen your skills and put you in the best shape of your life. Visit www.trainright.com

USA CYCLING This is the governing body of competitive cycling in the United States. The USA Cycling Web site, www.usacycling.org, has all the information you need to purchase a racing license and to find out where to use it.

always keep one complete riding kit organized and ready. That way, you can minimize the time you need to get out the door and maximize your riding.

3. PERFORM PREVENTIVE MAINTENANCE

Don't wait until you're halfway through the hour ride that you're squeezing in on a Wednesday afternoon to figure out that you have a cut in the sidewall of your rear tire. One evening each week, when your kids are in bed or you're too exhausted to do any other kind of work, carefully clean your bike with a dry towel and a citrus-based degreaser. As you wipe away the grime from your past week's rides, be sure to look carefully for dents, dings, or other irregularities in the frame and cuts in the tires or cracks in any components. Once you've wiped down the entire bike, be sure to use a light lube on the chain and inflate the tires to the correct pressure.

4. CARRY WHAT YOU NEED

Whether it's a college exam, an afternoon meeting at work, or your child's soccer game, coming home late from a ride because you got lost or had a "mechanical" you couldn't repair is no longer an option. The key is to keep a saddle bag on your bike with the basic tools you need to repair the most common mechanical mishaps. This includes a tube, tire levers, a pump or CO_2, a mini-tool (with a chain breaker), and a few dollars for emergencies. Needless to say, make sure that you and your kids know how to fix a flat, reassemble a broken chain, and troubleshoot any of the other common mechanical failures. Having the tools without knowing how to use them doesn't make a whole lot of sense.

5. KNOW YOUR ROUTE

If you have 2 hours to ride, you don't want to spend a quarter of your time figuring out your route or return an hour late because you lost your way. It's best to develop a number of rides of varying lengths that you can choose from based on the amount of time you have available. For example, a few different hour-long rides, one or two hour-and-a-half spins, and one really great 2-hour loop will give you a perfect selection to draw from. Use the days when you're not under tight time constraints to explore and develop new routes.

6. LET SOMEONE KNOW WHERE YOU'RE GOING

As you've learned by your twenties, life is somewhat less than predictable. So, always let someone know the route or general area that you're riding, what time you're leaving, and when you plan to return. That way, if you have a mechanical or fall, figuring out your whereabouts will be easier. It's important to tell someone before you leave because even in this age of widespread cell phone use, many of the best areas to ride are those that simply don't have mobile service.

7. MAKE THE MOST OF EVERY MINUTE

Once you're out the door and on your bike, *be* on your bike. Forget about your troubles at work, the bills that are sitting on your table, or appointments that you have later in the day. Riding is the time to relax and lose yourself in the physical act of exercise. Many times, the sheer act of letting go of the most obvious stresses in your life will lead you to answers to life's bigger questions.

GLOSSARY OF CYCLING TERMS

Abandon To pull out during a race or ride.

Aerobic Exercise at an intensity that allows the body's need for oxygen to be continually met. Aerobic exercise can be sustained for long periods of time. Cycling, for example, is great aerobic exercise.

ANSI American National Standards Institute, one of the groups responsible for certifying helmet testing standards.

Apex Sharpest part of a turn, where the transition from entering to exiting takes place.

Arc-en-ciel French word for "rainbow"; those color bands are represented on the jersey bestowed on a world champion.

ATB Acronym for "all-terrain bicycle"; used for mountain bikes.

Attack To accelerate or sprint away from other cyclists.

Axle Central axis for wheel or crank, it always rides on bearings or bushings.

Bail *(v., n.)* To crash, or the act of jumping or being thrown off a bike during a crash.

Ball bearings Spheres, usually made from steel, that allow a wheel or other part to turn easily.

Base Period of training to build general strength and fitness. It consists of long, often slow or steady riding.

Bead The edge along each side of a tire that snaps into a corresponding channel on the rim to hold the tire in place.

Beater A worn-out bicycle used for errands or other nonessential tasks.

Bike-a-thon A fund-raising bike tour.

Block To intentionally impede the progress of another cyclist during a race or competition.

Blow up To suddenly be unable to continue at a high pace due to over-exertion.

BMX Bicycle motocross; common name given to 20-inch-wheeled bikes with knobby tires.

Boneshaker Name given to the original velocipede, highlighting its jarring ride. (The velocipede was the predecessor of the bicycle, introduced in the Victorian age.)

Bonk To use all of your body's easily accessed energy, namely, stored glycogen. Bonking is a common cycling term for a variety of symptoms caused by low blood sugar, such as extreme exhaustion, mental confusion, hallucinations, being "out of it," or passing out.

Boot A small piece of material used inside a tire to cover a cut in the tread sidewall.

Bottom bracket Part where the crankset is installed. Also the axle, cups, and bearings of the crankset.

Breakaway One or more cyclists riding ahead of and separate from a main group.

Bridge To ride from one group of cyclists to another group that is ahead.

Brodie The act of skidding the rear wheel of a bike, often creating a large plume of dust.

Bunch A pack or field of cyclists.

Bunnyhop The act of making bike and rider airborne by pulling directly upright.

Cadence Rate of pedal rotation measured in revolutions per minute.

Carbohydrate loading A time-honored method for increasing energy reserves in advance of a demanding event.

Carve To corner especially hard on- or off-road.

Cassette Set of gears or cogs on the rear hub; formerly called a free-wheel.

Catch air When both wheels leave the ground while riding.

Century A 100-mile ride or event; a metric century is 100 kilometers, or 62 miles.

Chainring A sprocket on the crankset. There can be anywhere from one to three rings on a standard crankset.

Chainsuck When the chain sticks between the crankset and the frame; usually due to improper function of the chain.

Chamois Traditionally, a goatskin pad sewn into cycling shorts; synthetic materials have now replaced natural leather.

Clean *(adj.)* In mountain biking, when a rider makes it through a technically difficult section without putting his foot down.

Clincher The dominant bicycle tire type, it uses a separate tube and tire.

Clipless A pedal with a mechanical retention device similar to a ski binding.

Clunker Name given to homemade off-road bikes used by mountain biking pioneers; also a name for a well-worn bike.

CO_2 A compressed air cartridge used to inflate a flat tire in an emergency.

Coast To glide along while not pedaling.

Cog A sprocket mounted on the rear wheel; typical bikes feature anywhere from one to 10 cogs.

Criterium Multilap bike race on a short course (generally under 1 mile), often held in an urban area.

Cyclocross A type of off-road racing that combines running and riding over a short course with barriers and other obstacles.

Dab To put a foot down to prevent falling over.

Downhill/DH *(v., adj.)* To ride downhill, or a downhill race.

Downshift To shift to a lower gear—a larger cog or a smaller chainring.

Drafting To ride close behind another cyclist for aerodynamic advantage.

Drivetrain Components directly involved with making the rear wheel turn; includes the chain, crankset, shifters, cassette, rear derailleur, and front derailleur.

Drop, dropped *(v, adj.)* To lose contact with a group of riders.

Duathlon An event that combines running and cycling; also called a biathlon.

Echelon The type of paceline used when a large group of cyclists is riding into a crosswind.

Electrolytes Substances such as sodium, potassium, and chloride that are necessary for muscle contraction and maintenance of fluid levels.

Endo When a rider flips over the handlebars or has the rear wheel come off the ground.

Ergometer Stationary, bicycle-like device with adjustable pedal resistance used in physiological testing or for indoor training.

Field Main group of cyclists in a race or competition.

Fire road Wide dirt or gravel trail originally built to allow access for emergency vehicles, but commonly used for off-road riding.

Fixed gear Type of bicycle with a single gear and direct drive that does not allow for coasting or freewheeling. Commonly used on velodromes or bicycle racing tracks.

Flat tire When a tire loses its ability to retain air, usually due to a cut or abrasion in the inner tube.

Flyer Short-lived breakaway from a rider or group of riders during a race or competition.

Freeriding A style of mountain biking that involves large jumps, drops, and manmade stunts such as elevated bridges and life-size teeter-totters.

Freewheel The part of the bicycle that allows a rider to coast along without pedaling; also, the act of coasting.

Glutes Gluteal muscles of the buttocks. They are a key source of pedaling power.

Glycogen Fuel derived as glucose (sugar) from carbohydrates and stored in the muscles and liver. A primary source of energy for high-intensity cycling.

Glycogen window The period within an hour after exercise in which depleted muscles are most receptive to restoring their glycogen content. By eating foods or drinking fluids rich in carbohydrates, energy stores and recovery are enhanced.

Gradient Measure of the steepness of a road or trail, shown as a percentage.

Granny gear Small gear designed to make pedaling up steep hills possible.

Hammer To ride with great effort and zeal.

Hardtail A mountain bike without rear suspension.

Headset The parts on the top and bottom of the frame's headtube into which the handlebar, stem, and fork are fitted.

Headwind A wind that blows directly into the face of a rider.

Horsepower Measure of power output.

HPV Common abbreviation for human-powered vehicle.

Huck Slang for going off a jump or obstacle.

Hybrid A bike that combines the features of road and mountain bikes.

IMBA Abbreviation for International Mountain Bicycling Association.

Indoor trainer A stationary device that holds a standard bicycle for riding indoors or for warming up before a competition.

Intervals A structured method of training that alternates brief, hard efforts with short periods of easier riding or recovery.

Jam Another word for interval.

Jersey A technical shirt or top worn by a cyclist.

Jump Quick acceleration, usually standing on the pedals, out of the saddle.

Knobby A tire with raised bumps made especially for off-road riding.

Lactate threshold The exertion level beyond which the body can no longer produce energy aerobically, resulting in a buildup of lactic acid. Marked by muscle pain and fatigue.

Maillot jaune French term for the jersey awarded to the race leader of the Tour de France.

Mass start A race where multiple riders all begin and compete at one time.

Max VO$_2$ The maximum amount of oxygen that can be consumed during all-out exertion. This is a key indicator of a person's potential in cycling and other aerobic sports.

MTB Traditional abbreviation for mountain bike.

NORBA Abbreviation for National Off-Road Bicycle Association.

Off the back When a rider is dropped by another rider or group of riders.

Overgear To ride with a gear ratio that is too big for the terrain or the given fitness of a particular rider.

Overtraining Deep-seated fatigue, both physical and mental, caused by training at an intensity or volume too great for adaptation.

Oxygen debt The amount of oxygen that must be consumed to pay back the deficit incurred by anaerobic exertion.

Pace Average speed over a given time or distance.

Paceline Formation in which cyclists rotate from front to back in order to allow riders to rest while one rider breaks the wind and sets the pace.

Pad Protective material in shorts; see also **Chamois**.

Peloton French word for a group of cyclists; also called a bunch, a field, or a pack.

Portage The carrying of bikes around a challenging obstacle such as a stream or ditch.

Power Measure of the rate of energy output, commonly expressed in watts.

Preload Amount of pressure constantly applied to the spring on a shock or fork; it determines the way suspension reacts to body input and changes in terrain.

Presta valve A skinny valve with a top that threads up and down, used on more expensive bicycles.

Pull To ride at the front of a group or paceline.

Quadriceps The large muscle in front of the thigh, the strength of which helps determine a cyclist's ability to pedal with power.

Rail To ride quickly and smoothly through a corner.

Road rash Abrasions caused by a fall or crash.

Schraeder valve A type of air valve used on low-pressure tubes such as those on a downhill mountain bike or cruiser.

Sew-up A high-performance tire with casing sewn around an inner tube; it must be glued onto the rim.

Singletrack A trail wide enough for one person, usually 5 feet wide or less.

Sitting in Using another cyclist's slipstream to conserve energy.

Slipstream Protection from the wind provided by one cyclist to another riding directly behind.

Snakebite Two tiny punctures in a tube caused by the tube being pinched between the rim and an external source such as a rock or curb.

Snap Quick acceleration.

Spin To pedal with low effort and a high cadence.

Stage race A multirace usually held over multiple days and often consisting of various types of races. The winner is the rider with the lowest elapsed time for all races (stages).

Switchback A sharp turn in a road or trail, generally on an incline.

Taco The act of bending a wheel severely.

Tandem A bicycle made to accommodate two riders at once.

Tempo Riding at an effort slightly less than maximum, but not quite easy.

Time trial A race against the clock in which individual riders or small teams of riders start at set intervals.

Trailhead The point of entry for a bike path or off-road trail.

Travel In suspension, this is the maximum distance that a shock or fork can compress. Expressed in inches or millimeters.

True To straighten a wheel by means of tightening or loosening the spokes with a small wrench.

Tweak To modify something slightly, or to accidentally damage something.

Unicycle A cycle with a single wheel.

Velodrome A special track built especially for bicycle racing, it generally features steep banking.

Wheelbase The distance between the front and rear axles.

Wheelie To ride with the front wheel off the ground; to "pop a wheelie."

Wind-up Steady acceleration to an all-out effort.

XC Cross-country mountain bike riding or racing.

CREDITS

Front cover: Photograph © INMAGINE

Page vi: Photograph courtesy of Moab Action Shots (www.moabactionshots.com)

Page 5: Photograph © Bill Reitzel

Page 16: Photograph © Michael Brinson/Getty Images

Page 29: Photograph © Marcus Lyon/Getty Images

Page 34: Photograph © Ryan McVay/Getty Images

Page 36: Photograph © Hilmar

Page 51: Photograph © Stockbyte

Page 80: Photograph © Veer

Page 87: Photograph © Zak Kendal/Getty Images

Page 91: Photograph © Francis Hammond/Getty Images

Page 119: Photograph courtesy of Tom Danielson/Discover Channel Pro Cycling

Page 125: Photograph © Bill Reitzel

Page 132: Photograph courtesy of George Hincapie/Discovery Channel Pro Cycling

Back cover: Photograph courtesy of Discovery Channel Pro Cycling

The following companies are active supporters of the Discovery Channel® Pro Cycling Team:

www.Giro.com

www.Nike.com

www.PowerBar.com

www.Shimano.com

www.Trekbikes.com

INDEX

Boldface page references indicate photographs.
Underscored references indicate boxed text.